FLORENTINE CODEX

Florentine Codex

General History of the Things of New Spain

FRAY BERNARDINO DE SAHAGÚN

Book 7 – The Sun, Moon, and Stars, and the Binding of the Years

Translated from the Aztec into English, with notes and illustrations

By

ARTHUR J. O. ANDERSON
SCHOOL OF AMERICAN RESEARCH

CHARLES E. DIBBLE
UNIVERSITY OF UTAH

IN THIRTEEN PARTS

PART VIII

With an Appendix consisting of the first five chapters of Book VII from the Memoriales con escolios

Chapter heading designs are from the Codex

Published by

The School of American Research and The University of Utah

Monographs of The School of American Research

Number 14, Part VIII   Santa Fe, New Mexico   1953

CONTENTS

SEVENTH BOOK

Page

First Chapter, which telleth of the sun................................. 1

Second Chapter, which telleth of the moon........................... 3

Third Chapter, which telleth of the stars............................ 11

Fourth Chapter, which telleth of the stars........................... 13

Fifth Chapter, which telleth of the clouds........................... 17

Sixth Chapter. Here are mentioned the snow, the clouds, and the hail..... 19

The Seventh Chapter telleth of the year counter and the year sign........ 21

The Eighth Chapter telleth how they held in dread hunger and famine when One Rabbit ruled the year count, and what they first did when the year count of One Rabbit had not yet begun.................... 23

Ninth Chapter, in which is described what was called "The Binding of Our Years," or "When the Years are Bound," [which occurred] when one by one the four year signs had reigned thirteen years and when fifty-two years had passed; and what then was done......................... 25

Tenth Chapter, wherein is described the disposition of those who kept watch when the new fire appeared................................ 27

Eleventh Chapter, in which is told what they did when it was seen and was evident that the new fire burst out................................ 29

Twelfth Chapter, in which is told [the manner of conduct of] all the people when the new fire was taken. And, when this took place, everyone renewed his clothing and all the household goods................ 31

Appendix: Text of Sahagún's Memoriales con Escolios, *Comprising a Part of Book VII*... 33

First Chapter, of the sun.. 34

Second Chapter 38

Third Chapter, of the stars called Castor and Pollux.................... 60

Fourth Chapter 64

Fifth Chapter 72

LIST OF ILLUSTRATIONS

following page 38

Page from *Florentine Codex* (Chapter 12)

Page from *Memoriales con escolios* (Chapter 2)

1. Sun

2. Moon

3. The rabbit in the moon

4. Eclipse of the moon

5. Comet

6. Comet's tail

7. Stars

8. The winds

9–10. Lightning

11. Clouds

12. Rainbow

13. Ice, snow, and hail

14. Storing food against famine

15. Delivering children into bondage

16. Boring new fire on the breast of a sacrificial victim

17. New fire in the temples

18. New fire taken to homes

19. Breaking and throwing away household goods at the end of the fifty-two-year cycle

20. The calendar wheel

21–22. Sun, moon, stars, and other natural phenomena, from *Primeros Memoriales,* Cap. 2.

BOOK SEVEN--THE SUN, MOON, AND STARS, AND THE BINDING OF THE YEARS

Libro septimo, que trata
de la astrologia, y philo
sophia natural; que
alcançaron, estos
naturales, de
esta nueua
españa

De la astrologia

SEVENTH BOOK, WHICH TELLETH OF THE SUN, AND THE MOON, AND THE STARS;[1] AND OF [THE CEREMONY] OF THE BINDING OF THE YEARS.

JNIC CHICOME AMOSTLI, ITECHPA TLATOA IN TONATIUH: YOAN IN METZTLI, YOAN IN ÇIÇITLALTI, YOAN IN TOXIMMOLPIA.

First Chapter, which telleth of the sun.

The sun: the soaring eagle,[2] the turquoise prince, the god.

He shone, cast forth light, sent forth rays [of light] from himself. Hot, he burned men—he burned them exceedingly, and made them sweat. He turned men's skins brown, darkening them, blackening them, blistering them.

Every two hundred and sixty days, when his feast day came, then his festival was honored and celebrated. They observed it on his day sign, called Naui olin. And before his feast day had come, first, for four days, all fasted. And when it was already his feast day, when first he came forth, when he emerged and appeared, incense was offered and burned; blood [from the ears] was offered. This was done four times during the day—when it was dawn; and at noon; and past midday, when already [the sun] hung [low]; and when he entered [his house]—when he set; when he ended [his course].

And early in the morning it was said: "Now he will work; now the sun will labor. How will the day end?" And when night fell, it was said: "He hath worked; the sun hath labored." When he issued forth [at dawn], sometimes he was blood-colored, bright red, ruby-red. And sometimes he was quite pale, white-faced, pallid, because of the clouds—a mist, a

Inic ce capitulo, itechpa tlatoa: in tonatiuh.

Tonatiuh, quauhtleoanitl, xippilli, teutl.

Tona, tlanestia, motonameiotia: totonqui, tetlati, tetlatlati, teitoni: teistlileuh, teistlilo, teiscapotzo, teistlecaleuh.

Matlacpoaltica, ipan epoalli, in ilhuiuhquiçaia: in ilhuichiuililoia, ilhuiquistililoia: ipã quimattiuia, in itonal itoca naolin. Auh in aiamo quiça ilhuiuh: achtopa, nauilhuitl, neçaoaloia. Auh in icoac ie ipan ilhuiuh, in icoac iancuican, oalquiza, oalmomana, oalpetzini: tlenamacoia, tlatotonilo, neçoa. In hin, muchioaia nappa, cemilhuitl: icoac in ioatzinco, ioã nepãtla tonatiuh, ioan icoac in ie onmotzcaloa, in ie onmopiloa; ioã icoac in oncalaqui, in onaqui, in ommotzineoa.

Auh in ioatzinco, mitoaia: ca ie tequitiz, ie tlacotiz in tonatiuh; quen vetziz in cemilhuitl. Auh in oiooac, mitoaia: otequit, otlacotic in tonatiuh: inic oalmomana, in quenman uel eztic, chichiltic, tlapaltic. Auh in quenman, çan iztalectic çan camaztac, çan cocostiuh: ipampa in mistli, in mixaiauitl, anoço mispanitl, mistecuicuilli, in isco moteca.

---

1. The reader is referred to the *Memoriales con escolios,* in the Appendix to this book, taken from Francisco Paso y Troncoso, ed.: *Historia general de las cosas de Nueva España por Fray Bernardino de Sahagún: edición parcial en facsímile de los códices matritenses en lengua mexicana* (Madrid: Hauser y Menet, 1905).

2. *Quauhtleoanitl:* eagle with the fiery arrows, according to Rémi Siméon: *Dictionnaire de la langue nahuatl ou mexicaine* (Paris: Imprimerie Nationale, 1885).

heavy pall, or clouds of many colors—which were spread before his face.

Eclipse of the Sun

When this came to pass, he turned red; he became restless and troubled. He faltered and became very yellow. Then there were a tumult and disorder. All were disquieted, unnerved, frightened. There was weeping. The common folk raised a cry, lifting their voices, making a great din, calling out, shrieking. There was shouting everywhere. People of light complexion[3] were slain [as sacrifices]; captives were killed. All offered their blood; they drew straws through the lobes of their ears, which had been pierced. And in all the temples there was the singing of fitting chants; there was an uproar; there were war cries. It was thus said: "If the eclipse of the sun is complete, it will be dark forever! The demons of darkness will come down; they will eat men!"

Tonatiuh qualo.

Jn icoac muchioa, y, chichiliuhtimomana: aoc tlacamanj, aoc tlacaca, ca mocuecueptimanj: cēca tlacoçauia: niman ic tlatzomonj, tlacatl comonj: neacomanalo, necomonjlo, nemauhtilo, nechoquililo, tlachoquiztleoa in maceoalti: netenujteco, netempapaujlo, tlacaoaca, tlacaoatzalo, tzatzioa: oiooalli moteca, Tlacaztalmicoa, malmicoa, neçoa tlacoquistilo: nenacazteco: auh in teteupan, susuchcuico, tlachalantoc, tlacaoacatoc: ic mitoaia, intla tlamiz, in qualo tonatiuh: centlaiooaz: oaltemozque, in tzitzitzimi, tequaquiui.

---

3. *Tlacaztalmicoa:* cf., however, the corresponding passage in the *Memoriales con escolios* (Appendix to this volume), where the phrase is translated *"hombres de cabellos blancos y caras blancas."*

Second Chapter, which telleth of the moon.

The moon (Tecuciztecatl).

When he[4] newly appeared, he was like a small bow, like a bent, straw lip ornament—a small one. He did not yet shine. Very slowly, he went growing larger, becoming round and disc-shaped. In fifteen days he was completely rounded and filled out, as he became entire and mature. And when he waxed full and round, then he appeared, then he arose there at the place where the sun appeared. When it was already dark, [he was] like a very large, earthen skillet—very round, circular. [He was] as if red, a bright, deep red.

And after this, when he had already followed his course a little, when he had risen high, he became white. It was said: "Already he shineth; already the moon is brilliant; already he giveth forth moonbeams." He was then seen to be pale, very white. Then appeared [what was] like a little rabbit stretched across his face. If there were no clouds, if it were not overcast and covered by clouds, like [the sun] he shone, and it was like daytime. It was said: "[It is] almost [like] day; everywhere it is bright. Light is spread everywhere."

And when he had completely reached and attained his brilliance, for as many days as he had thus waxed and been round, little by little he again grew small; he became smaller. Again he became as when he had newly appeared. Gradually he waned and proceeded to vanish. It was said: "Already the moon is dying; now he slumbereth soundly—he falleth into a deep sleep. It is already toward morning, near dawn, when he ariseth." And when he had completely disappeared, it was said: "The moon hath died."

BEHOLD THE FABLE in which it is told how a little rabbit lay across the face of the moon. Of this, it is told that [the gods] were only at play with [the

Inic vme capitulo, itechpa tlatoa: in metztli.

Metztli. tecuciztecatl.

In icoac iancuican, oalmomana coltontli: iuhquin teçacanecuilli, teçacanecuiltontli, aiamo tlanestia: çan iuiian, ueistiuhi, malacachiuhtiuhi, teuilacachiuhtiuhi. Castoltica, in vel malacachiui: teuilacachiui, in vel maci, in chicaoa. Auh in icoac, vel oiaoaliuh, omalacachiuh, inic uel neci: inic oalmomana, in ompa iquiçaian tonatiuh: in jcoac ie tlapoiaoa, iuhquin comalli, veipol: vel teuilacachtic, malacachtic: iuhquin tlapalli, chichiltic, chichilpatic.

Auh quinjcoac, in ie achi quioaltoca, in ie, oalacoquiza, iztaia: mitoa ie tlachia, ie tlanestia, in metztli, ie metztona: iztalectic, vel iztac, inic motta: inic neci, iuhquin tochtõ, isco vetztoc: intlacamo tle mistli, intlacamo missoa, mistemi: iuhquin tona, ic tlaneci, mitoa ieh on cemilhuitl, uel tlanaltona: tlanaltonatimani.

Auh in jcoac, ouelacic, ouelmacic, itlanestiliz: in izquilhuitl, ic veiia, malacachiui: çan iuh nenti, oc ceppa tepitonaui, tepitonauhtiuhi, oc ceppa iuhqui muchioa, inic iancuican oalmomana: çan iuiian poliui, poliuhtiuhi: mitoa ie onmiqui, in metztli: ie uei in quicochi: ie ue in ic cochi, ie tlathuitiuhi, ie tlathuinaoac, in oalquiza. Auh in iquac uel ompoliuh, mitoa: ommic in metztli.

IZCATQUI, ITLATLATOLLO, inic mitoa: iuhquin tochton, isco uetztoc metztli. Jn hin, quilmach çã ic ica onneauiltiloc: ic conjsuiuitecque: ic conjstlatlatzoque,

4. In the Spanish version, the moon *(luna)* is feminine. Since both the sun (Nanauatzin) and moon (Tecuciztecatl) are male in the fable of the rabbit and the moon, we have made both of these consistently masculine.

moon]. They struck his face with [the rabbit]; they wounded his face with it—they maimed it. The gods thus dimmed his face. Thereafter [the moon] came to arise and come forth.

It is told that when yet [all] was in darkness, when yet no sun had shone and no dawn had broken—it is said—the gods gathered themselves together and took counsel among themselves there at Teotihuacan. They spoke; they said among themselves:

"Come hither, O gods! Who will carry the burden? Who will take it upon himself to be the sun, to bring the dawn?"

And upon this, one of them who was there spoke: Tecuciztecatl presented himself. He said: "O gods, I shall be the one."

And again the gods spoke: "[And] who else?"

Thereupon they looked around at one another. They pondered the matter. They said to one another: "How may this be? How may we decide?"

None dared; no one else came forward. Everyone was afraid; they [all] drew back.

And not present was one man, Nanauatzin; he stood there listening among the others to that which was discussed. Then the gods called to this one. They said to him: "Thou shalt be the one, O Nanauatzin."

He then eagerly accepted the decision; he took it gladly. He said: "It is well, O gods; you have been good to me."

Then they began now to do penance. They fasted four days—both Tecuciztecatl [and Nanauatzin]. And then, also, at this time, the fire was laid. Now it burned, there in the hearth. They named the hearth *teotexcalli.*

And this Tecuciztecatl: that with which he did penance was all costly. His fir branches [were] quetzal feathers, and his grass balls [were] of gold; his maguey spines [were] of green stone; the reddened, bloodied spines [were] of coral. And his incense was very good incense. And [as for] Nanauatzin, his fir branches were made[5] only of green water rushes— green reeds bound in threes, all [making], together, nine bundles. And his grass balls [were] only aromatic reeds. And his maguey spines were these same maguey spines. And the blood with which they were covered [was] his own blood. And [for] his incense, he used only the scabs from his sores, [which] he lifted up. For these two, for each one singly, a hill was made. There they remained, performing pen-

ic conjspopoloque: ic conjsomictique in teteuh: in icoac çatepan oquiçaco, omomanaco.

Mitoa, in oc iooaian, in aiamo tona, in aiamo tlathui: quilmach, mocentlalique, mononotzque, in teteuh: in vmpa teutiuacan, quitoque: quimolhuique.

Tla xioalhuiiã, teteuie: aquin tlatquiz? aquin tlamamaz? in tonaz, in tlathuiz?

Auh niman, ie ic iehoatl vncan ontlatoa: onmisquetza in tecuciztecatl, quito. Teteuie, ca nehoatl niiez:

Oc ceppa quitoque in teteu: aquin oc ce?

Niman ie ic nepanotl, mohotta: quimottitia, quimolhuia, quen on yez, y? quen toniezque?

Aiac motlapaloaia, in oc ce onmisquetzaz: çan muchi tlacatl momauhtiaia, tzinquiçaia.

Auh amo onnezticatca: in ce tlacatl nanaoatzin, vncan tehoan tlacacticatca, in nenonotzalo: nimã ic iehoatl, connotzque in teteu: quilhuique. Tehoatl tiiez, nanaoatze.

Niman quicuitiuetz, in tlatolli: quipaccaceli. Quito, Ca ie qualli teteuie: oannechmocnelilique.

Niman ic conpeoaltique, in ie tlamaceoa: moçauhque nauilhuitl: omextin in tecuciztecatl. Auh niman no icoac, motlali in tletl: ie tlatla, in vncan tlecuilco: quitocaiotia in tlecuilli, teutescalli.

Auh in iehoatl, tecuciztecatl, in ipan tlamaceoaia: muchi tlaçotli, imacxoiauh quetzalli, auh in içacatapaiol teucuitlatl, in ivitz chalchiuitl: inic tlaezuilli, tlaezçotilli, tapachtli: auh in icopal vel ieh in copalli. Auh in nanaoatzin, in jacxoiauh, muchi çan aacatl xoxouhqui, acaxoxouhqui, eey tlalpilli: tlacuitlalpilli, nepan chicunaui, in ie muchi: auh in içacatapaiol, çan ieeh in ocoçacatl: auh in iuitz, çan ie no ieh in meuitztli: auh inic quezhuiaia, uel ieh in iezço: auh in icopal, çan ieh in inanaoauh concocoleoaia. In imomestin y, cecentetl intepeuh muchiuh: in vmpa, ontlamaceuhtinenca: nauhiooal, mitoa in ascan, tetepe tzacuilli, itzacuil tonatiuh, yoan itzacoal metztli.

---

5. The corresponding passage in the *Memoriales con escolios* has *mochiuh* where the *Florentine Codex* has *muchi.*

ances for four nights. They are now called pyramids —the pyramid of the sun and the pyramid of the moon.

And when they ended their four nights of penitence, then they went to throw down and cast away, each one, their fir branches, and, indeed, all with which they had been performing penances. This was done at the time of their lifting [of the penance]; when, well into the night, they were to do their labor; they were to become gods.

And when midnight had come, thereupon [the gods] gave them their adornment; they arrayed them and readied them. To Tecuciztecatl they gave his round, forked heron feather headdress and his sleeveless jacket. But [as for] Nanauatzin, they bound on his headdress of mere paper and tied on his hair, called his paper hair. And [they gave him] his paper stole and his paper breech clout.

And when this was done, when midnight had come, all the gods proceeded to encircle the hearth, which was called *teotexcalli*, where for four days had burned the fire. On both sides [the gods] arranged themselves in line, and in the middle they set up, standing, these two, named Tecuciztecatl and Nanauatzin. They stood facing and looking toward the hearth.

And thereupon the gods spoke: They said to Tecuciztecatl: "Take courage, O Tecuciztecatl; fall —cast thyself—into the fire!"

Upon this, he went [forward] to cast himself into the flames. And when the heat came to reach him, it was insufferable, intolerable, and unbearable; for the hearth had blazed up exceedingly, a great heap of coals burned, and the flames flared up high. Thus he went terrified, stopped in fear, turned about, and went back. Then once more he set out, in order to try to do it. He exerted himself to the full, that he might cast and give himself to the flames. And he could in no way dare to do it. When again the heat reached him, he could only turn and leap back. He could not bear it. Four times indeed—four times in all—he was thus to act and try; then no more could he cast himself into the fire. For then [he could undertake it] only four times.

And when he had ended [trying] four times, thereupon they cried out to Nanauatzin. The gods said to him: "Onward, thou, O Nanauatzin! Take heart!"

And Nanauatzin, daring all at once, determined

Auh in ontzonquiz, nauhiooal intlamaceoaliz: niman quitlatlaçato, quimamaiauito, in imacxoiauh: yoan in ie muchi, ipan otlamaceuhque. Inin muchiuh, ie inneeoalco, in icoac in ie oaliooa tlacotizque, teutizque.

Auh in icoac, ie onaci iooalnepantla: niman ie ic quintlamamaca, quinchichioa, quincencaoa: in tecuciztecatl, quimacaque, iaztacon mimiltic, ioan ixicol. Auh in nanaoatzin, çan amatl, inic conquailpique: contzonilpique, itoca iamatzon: yoan iamaneapanal, yoan iamamastli.

Auh in ie iuhqui, in ouelacic ioalnepantla, in muchintin teteu quiiaoalotimomanque in tlecuilli, in moteneoa teutescalli, in vncan nauilhuitl otlatlac tletl, nenecoc motecpanque: auh nepantla quimõmanque quimonquetzque in omextin, y, moteneoa in tecuciztecatl yoan nanaoatzin, quisnamictimomanque, quisnamictimoquetzque in tlecuilli.

Auh niman ie ic tlatoa in teteu, quilhuique in tecuciztecatl. O tlacuelle tecuciztecatle, xonhuetzi, xonmomaiaui in tleco:

niman ie ic iauh momaiauiz in tleco. Auh in itech oacito totonillotl in amo isnamiquiztli, in amo iecoliztli, amo ihiouiliztli: inic cenca uel oxoxotlac tlecuilli, ovel oahoalantimotlali, ouel motlatlali in tletl: ic çan ommismauhtito, ommotilquetzato, oaltzinquiz, oaltzinilot: ie no ceppa iauh tlaiehecoz, isquich ca ana, ic momotla, quimomaca in tletl: auh ça auel motlapalo, in ie no itech onaci totonqui, çan oaltzinquiça oaltzincholoa, amo ontlaiecoa: uel nappa, tlaelnappa in iuh quichiuh in moieheco, çã niman auel ommomaiauh in tleco: ca çan ie vncan tlateneoalli in nappa.

Auh in ontlaquisti nappa: niman ie ic ieh contzatzilia in nanaoatzin, quilhuique in teteu. Oc tehuatl, oc cuel tehoatl nanaoatze, ma ie cuel.

Auh in nanaoatzin, çan cen in oalmotlapalo, qui-

5

—resolved—hardened his heart, and shut firmly his eyes. He had no fear; he did not stop short; he did not falter in fright; he did not turn back. All at once he quickly threw and cast himself into the fire; once and for all he went. Thereupon he burned; his body crackled and sizzled.

And when Tecuciztecatl saw that already he burned, then, afterwards, he cast himself upon [the fire]. Thereupon he also burned.

And thus do they say: It is told that then flew up an eagle, [which] followed them. It threw itself suddenly into the flames; it cast itself into them, [while] still it blazed up. Therefore its feathers are scorched looking and blackened. And afterwards followed an ocelot, when now the fire no longer burned high, and he came to fall in. Thus he was only blackened —smutted—in various places, and singed by the fire. [For] it was not now burning hot. Therefore he was only spotted, dotted with black spots, [as if] splashed with black.

From this [event], it is said, they took—from here was taken—the custom whereby was called and named one who was valiant, a warrior. He was given the name *quauhtlocelotl*. [The word] *quauhtli* came first, it is told, because, [as] was said, [the eagle] first entered the fire. And the ocelot followed thereafter. Thus is it said in one word—*quauhtlocelotl*; because [the latter] fell into the fire after [the eagle].

And after this, when both had cast themselves into the flames, when they had already burned, then the gods sat waiting [to see] where Nanauatzin would come to rise—he who first fell into the fire—in order that he might shine [as the sun]; in order that dawn might break.

When the gods had sat and been waiting for a long time, thereupon began the reddening [of the dawn]; in all directions, all around, the dawn and light extended. And so, they say, thereupon the gods fell upon their knees in order to await where he who had become the sun would come to rise. In all directions they looked; everywhere they peered and kept turning about. As to no place were they agreed in their opinions and thoughts. There was dissension when they spoke. Some thought that it would be from the north that [the sun] would come to rise, and placed themselves to look there; some [did so] to the west; some placed themselves to look south. They expected [that he might rise] in all directions, because the light was everywhere.

oalcentlami, quioallancoa in iiollo, oalistetenmotzolo: amo tle ic mismauhti, amo moquehquetz, amo motilquetz, amo tzinquiz: çan niman ommotlaztiuetz, õmomaiauhtiuetz in tleco, çan ic cenia: niman ie ic tlatla, cuecuepoca, tzotzoioca in inacaio.

Auh in icoac, oquittac tecuciztecatl, in ie tlatla: quinicoac, çatepan ipan onmomaiauh: niman ie no ic tlatla.

Auh in iuh conitoa, quilmach niman no ic oneoac, in quauhtli, quimontoquili: onmotlaztiuetz in tleco, ommotlecomaiauh, oc iehoatl no vellalac: ipampa in iuiio cuicheoac, cuichectic. Auh ça ontlatzacui in ocelotl, aocmo cenca uellala in tletl, uetzito: ic ça motlecuicuilo, motletlecuicuilo, motlechichino, aocmo cenca uellalac: ipampan çan cuicuiltic, motlilchachapani, motlilchachazpatz.

In hin, quilmach vncan man, vncan mocuic in tlatolli: inic itolo, teneoalo, in aquin tiacauh, oquichtli: quauhtlocelotl tocaiotilo: ieh iacattiuh in quauhtli, mitoa, quil ipampa in onteiacan tleco: auh ça ontlatzacuia in ocelotl, inic mocencamaitoa quauhtlocelotl: ipampa i çatepã ouetz tleco.

Auh in ie iuhqui, in omestin õmomamaiauhque tleco, in icoac ie otlatlaque: niman ic quichistimotecaque in teteu, in campa ic quiçaquiuh nanaoatzin, in achto onuetz tleco: inic tonaz, inic tlathuiz.

In icoac ie uecauhtica onoque, mochiscaonoque teteu: nimã ie ic peoa, in tlachichiliui, nouiiampa tlaiaoalo in tlauizcalli, in tlatlauillotl: in iuh conitoa, niman ie ic motlanquaquetzque in teteu, inic quichiezque, in campa ie quiçaquiuh tonatiuh. Omuchiuh, nouiiampa tlachisque, auicpa tlachie, momalacachotinemi: acan vel centetis in intlatol, in innemachiliz, atle i uel iaca in quitoque. Cequintin momatque, ca mictlampa in quiçaquiuh, ic vmpa itztimomanque: cequintin cioatlampa: cequintin vitztlampa itztimomanque, nouiiampa motemachique: ipampa in çan tlaiaoalo tlatlauillotl.

6

And some placed themselves so that they could watch there to the east. They said: "For there, in that place, the sun already will come to arise." True indeed were the words of those who looked there and pointed with their fingers in that direction. Thus they say, [that] those who looked there [to the east were] Quetzalcoatl; the name of the second was Ecatl; and Totec, or Anauatl itecu; and the red Tezcatlipoca. Also [there were] those who were called the Mimixcoa, who were without number; and four women—Tiacapan, Teicu, Tlacoyehua, and Xocoyotl.

And when the sun came to rise, when he burst forth, he appeared to be red; he kept swaying from side to side. It was impossible to look into his face; he blinded one with his light. Intensely did he shine. He issued rays of light from himself; his rays reached in all directions; his brilliant rays penetrated everywhere.

And afterwards Tecuciztecatl came to rise, following behind him from the same place—the east,—near where the sun had come bursting forth. In the same manner that they had fallen into the fire, just so they came forth. They came following each other.

And so they tell it; [so] they relate the story and repeat the legend: Exactly equal had they become in their appearance, as they shone. When the gods saw them, [thus] exactly the same in their aspect, then once more there was deliberation. They said: "How may this be, O gods? Will they perchance both together follow the same path? Will they both shine like this?"

And the gods all issued a judgment. They said: "Thus will this be; thus will this be done."

Then one of the gods came out running. With a rabbit he came to wound in the face this Tecuciztecatl; with it he darkened his face; he killed its brilliance. Thus doth it appear today.

And when this was done, when both appeared [over the earth] together, they could, on the other hand, not move nor follow their paths. They could only remain still and motionless. So once again the gods spoke: "How shall we live? The sun cannot move. Shall we perchance live among common folk? [Let] this be, that through us the sun may be revived. Let all of us die."

Auh in cequintin, vel vmpa itztimomãque in tlauhcopa: quitoque. Ca ie vmpa hin, ie vncan hin in quiçaquiuh tonatiuh: iehoantin uel neltic in intlatol, in vmpa tlachisque, in vmpa mapiloque. Iuh quitoa, iehoantin in vmpa tlachisque, quetzalcoatl: ic ontetl itoca hecatl, yoan in totec, anoço anoço anaoatl itecu, yoan tlatlauic tezcatlipuca: no iehoantin in moteneoa mimiscoa, in amo çã tlapoaltin: yoan cioa nauin, tiacapan, teicu, tlacoiehoa, xocoiotl.

Auh in jcoac, oquiçaco, in omomanaco tonatiuh: iuhquin tlapalli monenecuilotimanj, amo vel isnamico, teismimicti: cenca tlanestia, motonameiotia, in itonameio nouiiampa aacitimoquetz, auh in itonalmiio nouiiampa cacalac.

Auh çatepan, quiçaco in tecuciztecatl, quioaltocatia: çan ie no vmpa in tlauhcopa, itloc onmomanaco in tonatiuh: in iuh onuetzque tleco, çan no iuh oalquizque, oalmotocatiaque.

Auh in iuh conitoa, tlatlanonotza, teçaçanilhuia: çan neneuhqui in intlachieliz muchiuh, inic tlanestiaia. In icoac oquimittaque teteu, in çan neneuhqui intlachieliz: nimã ic no ceppa ic nenonotzalo: quitoque. Quen iezque, y, teteuie? cuis onteistin otlatocazque, onteistin iuh tlanestizque?

Auh in teteu, muchintin oallatzõtecque: quitoque. Iuh iez, y, iuh, muchioaz y.

Niman ic ce tlacatl, ommotlalotiquiz in teteu: ic conisuiuitequito in tochin, in iehoatl tecuciztecatl, ic conispopoloque, ic conisomictique: in iuhqui ascan ic tlachie.

Auh in ie iuhqui: in icoac ie omomanaco onteistin, ie no cuele auel olini, otlatoca, çan momanque, motẽmanque. Ic ie no ceppa quitoque in teteu. Quen tinemjzque, amo olinj in tonatiuh: cuis tiquinnelotinemjzque in maçeoalti? Auh inin, ma toca mozcalti, ma timuchintin timiquican.

7

Then it became the office of Ecatl to slay the gods. But they say thus: that Xolotl wished not to die. He said to the gods: "Let me not die, O gods." Wherefore he wept much; his eyes and his eyelids swelled.

And when death approached near unto him, he fled from its presence; he ran; he quickly entered a field of green maize, and took the form of, and quickly turned into, two young maize stalks [growing] from a single root, which the workers in the field have named *xolotl*. But there, in the field of green maize, he was seen. Then once again he fled from him; once more he quickly entered a maguey field. There also he quickly changed himself into a maguey plant [consisting of] two [parts] called *mexolotl*. Once more he was seen, and once more he quickly entered into the water and went to take the shape of [an amphibious animal called] *axolotl*. There they could go to seize him, that they might slay him.

And they say that though all the gods died, even then the sun god could not move and follow his path. Thus it became the charge of Ecatl, the wind, who arose and exerted himself fiercely and violently as he blew. At once he could move him, who thereupon went on his way. And when he had already followed his course, only the moon remained there. At the time when the sun came to enter the place where he set, then once more the moon moved. So, there, they passed each other and went each one his own way. Thus the sun cometh forth once, and spendeth the whole day [in his work]; and the moon undertaketh the night's task; he worketh all night; he doth his labor at night.

From this it appeareth, it is said, that the moon, Tecuciztecatl, would have been the sun if he had been first to cast himself into the fire; because he had presented himself first and all [his offerings] had been costly in the penances.

Here endeth this legend and fable, which was told in times past, and was in the keeping of the old people.

Eclipse of the Moon.

When the moon eclipsed, his face grew dark and sooty; blackness and darkness spread. When this came to pass, women with child feared evil; they thought it portentous; they were terrified [lest], perchance, their [unborn] children might be changed

Nimã ic ieh itequiuh õmochiuh, in hecatl, ie quinmjctia in teteu: auh in iuh conitoa, in xolotl, amo momiquitlania: quimilhui in teteu. Macamo nimiqui teteuie. Ic cẽca chocaia, vel ispopoçaoac, isquatolpopoçaoac.

Auh in ie itech onaci miquiztli, çan teispãpa eoac, cholo, toctitlan calactiuetz: ipan onmixeuh, ic mocueptiuetz, in toctli ome manj, maxaltic: in quitocaiotia millaca, xolotl. Auh vncan ittoc in toctitlan: ie no ceppa teispampa eoac, ie no cuele metitlan calactiuetz: no ic õmocueptiuetz in metl, ome manj, in itoca mexolotl. Ie no ceppa ittoc, ie no cuele atlan calactiuetz, axolotl mocuepato: ie vel vmpa canato, inic conmictique.

Auh quitoa, in manel muchintin teteu omicque, ça nel amo ic olin, amo vel ic otlatocac in teutl tonatiuh: ic itequiuh ommuchiuh in hecatl, moquetz in ehecatl, cenca molhui, totocac, in ehecac: quin iehoatl vel colinj, niman ie ic otlatoca. Auh in icoac, ie otlatoca, çan vmpa ommocauh in metztli: quinicoac in ocalaquito icalaquian tonatiuh, ie no cuele ic oaleoac in metztli: ic vncan mopatilique, motlallotique. Inic ceppa oalquiça tlacemilhuitiltia in tonatiuh: auh in metztli iooaltequitl quitlaça cẽiooal quitlaça, iooaltequiti.

Ic vncã hin neci, mitoa: ca iehoatl tonatiuh iezquia in metztli tecuciztecatl, intla ic achto onuetzinj tleco: ipampa ca iehoatl achto misquetz, inic muchi tlaçotli ipan tlamaceuh.

Nican tlami, in hin nenonotzalli, çaçanilli: in ie uecauh ic tlatlanonotzaia, veuetque, in impiel catca.

Metztli qualo.

In icoac, qualo metztli: istlileoa, iscuicheoa, cuicheoatimomana, tlaiooatimomana. In icoac, y, muchioa: uel motẽmatia in ootztin, tlaueimatia, momauhtiaia: ma nelli moquimichcuepti, ma quiquimichtinmocuepti, in impilhoan.

into mice; each of their children might turn into a mouse.

And because they feared evil, in order to protect themselves, in order that this might not befall [them], they placed obsidian in their mouths or in their bosoms, because with this their children would not be born with mouth eaten away—lipless; or they would not be born with noses eaten away or broken off; or with twisted mouths or lips; or cross-eyed, squint-eyed, or with shrunken eyes; nor would they be born monstrous or imperfect.

This moon those of Xaltocan worshipped as a god, and they laid offerings before him and paid him honor.

Auh inic quintemmatia: inic mopatiaia, inic amo iuhqui impã muchioaz: itztli incamac, anoço inxillã quitlaliaia: ipãpa inic amo tencoaiuizque, tencoatizque impilhoan: anoço iacacoatizque, iacacotonizque, anoço tempatziuizque, tennecuiliuizque, ispatziuizque, isnecuiliuizque, isoacaliuizque: in anoço atlacacemele tlacatiz, in amo tlacamelaoac.

Inin metztli, iehoan quimoteutiaia in xaltocameca: quitlamaniliaia, quimauiztiliaia.

Third Chapter, which telleth of the stars.

The Fire Drill[6]

When [these] appeared and set forth, incense was offered and burned. Thus was it said when Yoaltecutli [and] Yacauitztli had come forth: "What will the night bring? How will the day break?"

And these were offered incense. Three times was it done: when night fell—well into the night; and when it was time to sleep—the time when the flutes were blown.[7] When this [took place], this was the time for offering their blood and offering maguey spines stained with blood. The third time incense was offered was when it dawned, when the morning broke, when the earth was visible—when morning was near.

And hence was it said that they resembled the fire drill: because when fire was drawn with a drill, and the drill bored, thus fell, ignited, and flared the fire.

And also for this reason all burned [spots on] their wrists; for this reason were we men burned on the wrists, to show awe of him. He was feared and dreaded. It was said and considered of any whose wrists were not burned that on his wrists fire would be drilled in the land of the dead, when he died. Therefore we men—every one—were burned on the wrists. On both sides of each wrist they arranged in order, in rows, their wrist burns. Thus they represented the fire drill. In the same manner as [the stars] were arranged in order and in line, so also they placed in order, in rows, their burns on their wrists.

[The Morning Star or Great Star]

Of the morning star, the great star, it was said that when first it emerged and came forth, four times it vanished and disappeared quickly. And afterwards it burst forth completely, took its place in full light,

---

Inic ey capitulo, intechpa tlatoa: in cicitlaltin.

Mamalhoaztli.

In icoac oalneci, oalmotema: tlenamacoia, tlatotoniloia: ic mitoaia, ooaluetz in iooaltecutli, in iacauiztli: quen uetziz in iooalli, quen tlathuiz.

Auh in hin tlenamacoia, espa in muchioaia: icoac in tlapoiaoa, tlaquauhtlapoiaoa, yoan netetequizpan, tlatlapitzalizpa. Icoac, y, neçoaia, neuitzmanaloia: ic espa tlenamacoia, icoac in tlauizcaleoa, tlauizcalli moquetza: in tlatlalchipaoa, in ie tlathuinaoac.

Auh inic mitoa, mamalhoaztli, itech moneneuilia in tlequauitl: iehica, in icoac tlequauhtlaxo, ca momamali in tlequauitl: inic uetzi, inic xotla, inic mopitza tletl.

No yoan, inic nematlatiloia: inic momatlatiaia toquichtin, iehoatl quimacacia, mjmacacia imacaxoia, mjtoaia: quilmach in aquin amo nematlatile, imac tlequauhtlaxoz in mjctlan, in icoac omjc. Iehica in toquichtin, muchi tlacatl momatlatiaia, nenecoc inmac quiuiujpanaia, quitetecpanaia in innematlatil: ic quitlaiehecalhuiaia in mamalhoaztli: in iuh vipantoc, tecpantoc, no iuh quiuiuipanaia, quitetecpanaia in immac innematlatil.

Citlalpol, vei citlalin mitoa: in icoac iancuican oalcholoa, oalquiça, nappan poliui, popoliuhtiuetzi: auh çatepā uel cueponj, cuepontimotlalia, cuepontica, tlanestitica: iuhquin metztona ic tlanestia.

---

6. The names of various constellations and stars may or may not correspond to the names by which they are now known. In the Spanish text and in the *Memoriales con escolios*, however, Sahagún equates them with the terminology current in his times. See also Plates 1-7, 21.

7. *Tlatlapitzalizpan:* cf. Arthur J. O. Anderson and Charles E. Dibble: *Florentine Codex*, Book II, *The Ceremonies* (Santa Fe: School of American Research, Monograph No. 14, Part III, and University of Utah, 1951), p. 192; also Siméon, *op. cit.*; Angel María Garibay K: *Llave del náhuatl* (Otumba: [Imprenta Mayli, S.A.], 1940), p. 252. The ceremony called for use of flutes or trumpets, according to Siméon; of flutes, according to Garibay. Sources vary as to the exact time when these were blown.

became brilliant, and shone white. Like the moon's rays, so did it shine.

And when it newly emerged, much fear came over them; all were frightened. Everywhere the outlets and openings[8] [of houses] were closed up. It was said that perchance [the light] might bring a cause of sickness, something evil, when it came to emerge. But sometimes they regarded it as benevolent.

And also [captives] were slain when it emerged, [that] it might be nourished. They sprinkled blood toward it. With the blood of captives they spattered toward it, flipping the middle finger from the thumb; they cast [the blood] as an offering; they raised it in dedication.

Auh in icoac, iancuican oalcholoa: cĕca mauiztli motecaia, nemauhtiloia: nouiian motzatzacoaia in tlecalli, in puchquiiaoatl: mitoaia, aço cocolizço, itla aqualli quitquitiuitz, in oquiçaco: auh in quenman quicoalittaia.

Auh no micoaia, in icoac oalcholoa, izcaltiloia, quitlacoaliaia: imezçotica in mamalti, contlatzitzicuiniliaia, contlatlatlaxiliaia, contlaiiauiliaia.

8. The corresponding Spanish text translates these as doors and windows. Cf. Arthur J. O. Anderson and Charles E. Dibble: *Florentine Codex, Book III, The Origin of the Gods* (Santa Fe: School of American Research, Monograph No. 14, Part IV, and University of Utah, 1952), p. 39, n. 3a.

Fourth Chapter, which telleth of the stars.

The Comet

It was said [to be] an omen for the ruler. Because of it a ruler was to perish; perchance some person of noble lineage would die. And likewise they said that somewhere he might be imprisoned, or war would begin. Or else there would be famine. The common folk said: "Perhaps this is our hunger; perchance famine," they said.

The Shooting Star

It was said that the passing of a shooting star rose and fell neither without purpose nor in vain. It brought a worm to something. And of [the animal] wounded by a shooting star, they said: "It hath been wounded by a shooting star; it hath received a worm." [Such] was not to be eaten. It was looked at with fear, abhorred, and shunned. It turned one's stomach.

And by night all were well protected. All covered themselves; they clothed themselves, wrapped themselves in mantles, and bound on their garments, for fear of the shooting star.

The S-Shaped Stars

[These] were apart; they appeared by themselves, shining and shimmering. And for this reason were they called S-shaped stars—that they were similar to and very much like a [kind of maize] tortilla which was made, or an amaranth seed tortilla. [These] were, at both ends, twisted and rounded over. They were eaten on the day Xochitl, everywhere, in each house. It was done in all places; in men's dwellings everywhere, they were made.

The Scorpion Stars

In the same manner, [these] resembled and appeared in the aspect of the venomous scorpion, with upcurved tail. Arched and upcurled is its tail; wherefore [these] are called the Scorpion Stars.

Inic naui Capitulo, itechpa tlatoa: in cicitlaltin.

Citlalin popoca.

Mitoa: tlatocatetzauitl, ic tlatocamicoaz, aço aca uey tlaçopilli ie mjquiz: yoan no quitoaia, aço cana ie oalmotzacoaz, aço ie olinjz teuatl tlachinolli: yoan anoço ie maianaloz. Quitoaia in maceoalti: aço tapiz hi, aço apiztli quitoa.

Citlalin tlamina,

Mitoa: amo nenquiça, amo nĕuetzi, in itlamjnaliz: tlaocuillotia. Auh in tlamintli, mitoa: citlalmjnqui, ocuillo, aocmo qualo, mauhcaitto, tlaelitto, hihielo, tetlaieltia.

Auh in iooaltica vel nemalhuilo, neolololo, netlapacholo, nequentilo, netlalpililo: imacaxo in itlaminaliz citlalin.

Citlalsunecuilli.

Çan iioca onoc, iioca neztoc, tlanestitoc, cuecuepocatoc: Auh inic mitoa, citlalsunecuilli: ca quineneuilia, vel no iuhqui centlamantli tlachichioalli tlascalli, anoço tzooalli: nenecoc, cecentlapal quacoltic, quateuilacachtic: suchilhuitl ipan in quaqualoia, nouiian cecencalpan: quitzacutimanca, in nouiian techachan nechiuililoia.

Citlalcolotl.

Çan no iuhqui: quineneuilia, quinamiqui, in itlachieliz tequani colotl: cuitlapilcocoltic, mamalacachtic, teteuilacachtic in jcuitlapil: ipampa inic mitoa citlalcolotl.

The Wind

That which was known as [the wind] was addressed as Quetzalcoatl. From four directions it came, from four directions it traveled. The first place whence it came was the place from which the sun arose, which they named Tlalocan. This wind which came from there they gave the name of Tlalocayotl. Little did it frighten men; lightly did it blow. With it, one could go in a canoe; with it one could land; with it one could cross the water.

The second place whence it came [the north] was called Mictlampa; and this was named the wind from the land of the dead. This was much feared, and caused much terror. Violently did it blow, when it set in, and the canoes could not contend with it. They could not travel forward. They could not venture forth; they could not pass across; they could not get under way in the water. Rather, all the boatmen came out and left [their craft] because of fear—those who gained their livelihoods on the water, the fishermen who used nets, or who speared [the fish]. When they saw that it was Mictlampa ehecatl which arose, then they feared evil and were troubled. They hurried, hastened, and greatly quickened their pace, plying the pole—plying it rapidly. They strained their arms, that they might come out and beach [the canoe] on the shore, on the edge of the water, near the water line. And so they said: "Often it drowneth men and sinketh canoes."

The third place whence it came [the west] was known as Ciuatlampa; it was named Ciuatecayotl and Ciuatlampa ehecatl. Also it was called One Wind. or Maçaua; for it came from Maçauacan. And this one did not blow fiercely. Nevertheless, it was very cold. Men suffered much from [its] cold; they became livid and stiff from cold. It made them shiver; it was deadly. It made men tremble, shake, and quake; it exhausted them; it gave them stomach pains, or pains in the lungs, or the head. And yet, with it they could go ashore from the water. It did not frighten men nor terrify them.

And the fourth place whence came the wind [the south] was there from Uitztlampa. It was named Uitztlampa ehecatl. And this one was much feared and held in dread. All feared harm. It made men speechless with terror; it made them silent with fear. Because it blew swiftly, it frightened them greatly. They said: "When it ariseth, it uprooteth and breaketh trees: and it teareth walls to pieces—old walls

Ehecatl

Moteneoaia: ic quinotzaia quetzalcoatl. Nauhcampa oallauh, nauhcampa oalitztiuh. Inic ceccan oallauh: vmpa in iquiçaiampa tonatiuh, quitoaia tlalocã: inin ehecatl, vmpa oallauh, quitocaiotiaia, tlalocaiotl: amo cẽca temauhti, amo cenca totoca, uel ipan acaltica viloa, vel ipan quixoa, in atlan: vel ipã panoa.

Inic occã oallauh, moteneoa mictlampa: auh inin motocaiotia mictlampa ehecatl. In hin uel imacaxo, uellamauhtia: cenca totoca, in icoac moquetza, amo vel quisnamiqui in acalli: amo vellauilteco, amo uel tlastlapalolo, avel istlapal viloa, auel tlanecuilolo in atlan: çan mauhcaquixoa, mauhcaquiça in tlapanauique, in atlâca, in tlâtlamâque, in tlamjnque. In oquittaque, ca mictlampa ehecatl in omoquetz: ic cenca motenmati, motequipachoa, uel motequimati, ompilcatoque, ompipilcatoque, in tlaneloa, in tequitlaneloa: vel momaquauhtilia, inic uel onquiça, onmacana atenco, atexipalco, achichiiacpa: iuh quitoa, ca miecpa, teatlanmictia, quipolactia in acalli.

Inic escan oallauh: moteneoa cioatlãpa, motocaiotia, cioatecaiotl, cioatlampa ehecatl: no quitocaiotia ce ehecatl, anoço maçaoac ipampa vmpan oalitztiuh maçaoacan. Auh in hin, amo no cenca totoca: iece cenca itztic, uel tececmjti, tepineoalti, tepineuh, tetetziliuiti, tetetzilquisti, tetzitzilquiti, teuiuiioquilti, tecuecuechquiti, tecuecuechmiquiti: texillanquauhtili, teiomotlanquauhtili, tetzonteconeuh. Auh tel, uel ipan quixoa in atlan, amo temauhti, amo temauizcuiti.

Auh inic nauhcampa, oallauh ehecatl, vmpa uitztlampa: motocaiotia uitztlampa ehecatl. Auh inin, cenca vel imacaxo, mimacaci: netenmacho, aoc tenaoatilti, aoc tetlatolti: ipãpa cenca totoca, cenca tlamauhtia. Quitoa, in icoac moquetza: vel quitzjneoa, quipoztequi in quauitl: yoan quixitinja in tepantli, in tepançolli, in xacalli: quecatoctia in tlatzacuilli, in chinancalli. Auh in vei atl vel colinja, quiteponaçoa,

and straw huts. The wind carrieth off fences and enclosures. And it stirreth up the seas; it maketh them froth and foam. It formeth waves; there is a great din as of waves breaking. There is a great crackling noise." And it tossed and cast canoes into the air. Just so, indeed, did the north wind sink them.

Lightning; the Lightning Flash

They addressed it as, and named it, many things—the mist which went winding [like a serpent], the thunderbolt, the reed staff. When lighting flashed and lit up repeatedly, we were blinded, we lost our sight, our vision was darkened. It startled us; we were terrified. It was unbearable to look at; it was dazzling. Everywhere it flashed repeatedly—again and again—like the light of the dawn breaking over and over. Thus did it come; it came twisting and winding.

quipoçonaltia, cacuecueniotia: iuhquin tetecuicatimani, cocomocatimani: auh in acalli caacomaiaui, caacotlaça: vel no iuhqui, quinamiqui in mictlampa ehecatl.

Tlapetlanjllotl, Tlapetlanjliztli

much ic quinotzaia, quitocaiotiaia, aiauhcocolli, tlapetlanjlquauitl, oztopilcoauitl. In icoac tlapetlani, tlâtlapetlani: tispoiaoa, tismimiqui, titismauhtia, titocuitiuetzi: aisnamiquiliztli, aisnamiquiztli, nouiian tlatlaneztimoquetza: iuhquin tlauizcalli moquequetza: inic oallauh oalcocoliuhtiuh, cuecueliuhtiuitz.

Fifth Chapter, which telleth of the clouds.

The Lord of Tlalocan

He was considered a god. To him were attributed rain and water. Thus they said he made that which we ate and drank—food, drink, our sustenance, our nourishment, our daily bread, our maintenance. All that which grew in the summer [he made]—sprouts, fresh green sprouts, trees, amaranth, *chía*, squash, beans; the maguey, the tuna cactus; and still others, not edible—flowers, herbs.

And when his feast was observed, first there was fasting for four days. The priests fasted in honor of Tlaloc in what was called the priests' house, where they had matured and grown.

When the fourth day had passed, when the fasting had ended, when the feast had been completed, [the evildoers] were plunged and submerged repeatedly in the lake. Not soft, not gentle was the punishment. They were plunged and immersed repeatedly in the water. They ill-used only those of their own kind. They dragged [the victim] back and forth through the mud. They plunged him under the water and dragged him; they went pulling him along by the hair; they kicked him. [As] he swam under the water, churning, beating, and swirling it up as he went, he escaped the hands of the priests.

When a fault had been committed in the priests' house, or some error had been done—even though someone had only stumbled, or tripped over something, at once, for this, they laid hold of him. Because of it they shut him in as their captive, no more taking their eyes from him, that they might plunge him in the water.

And to excess did they set upon him. Greatly did they afflict and torment him. He lay half dead, breathing his last, gasping, in his last agonies; at death's door [was he] whom they finally cast on the shore. No one could plead his cause. From thence [the victims'] fathers and mothers took them. And if anyone felt apprehension or foreboding for his son, in order that [the priests] should not plunge him into the

Ic macuilli capitulo, itechpa tlatoa: in mistli.

Tlalocã tecutli,

Teutl ipan machoia, itech tlamiloia, in quiauitl, in atl: iuh quitoaia, ie quichioa in ticooa, in tiqui, in qualoni, in joani, in tonenca, in toiolca, in tocochca, in toneuhca, in tocemilhuitiaia, in tonacaiotl: in ie isquich xopaniotl, in itzmolintoc, in celiztoc, in quauitl, in oauhtli, in chian, in aiotetl, in etl, in metl, in nopalli: yoan in oc cequi, in amo qualoni, in suchitl, in xiuitl.

Auh in icoac ilhuiquistililoia: achtopa nauilhuitl moçaoaia, motlalocaçaoaia in tlamacazque: in moteneoa calmecac mooapaoa, mozcaltia.

In icoac oacic nauilhuitl, in ie neoalco, in ie ilhuitl muchioa: matlampapachoaia, mopopolactiaia in uei apan: amo iuiian, amo motlamachuja, in atlan onmotzotzopontitlaça, onmotzotzopontimaiaui: çan monetechuja, vncan çoquititlan quinemjtia, quipopolactia, quiuiuiuilana: icpac cantinemi, quititilicça, atlã tlatzotzopotztinemj, aicoxotztinemi, tlamomolotztinemi: inmac mouiuitlatinemi, in tlamacazque,

in otlatlaco, in calmecac itlâ oncholo: intlanel çan aca õmotepotlami, itlâ oconicxixopeuh, oc uel ic conacique, ie ic inmal ça quipipia, aocmo conjscaoa, inic catlampapachozque.

Auh amo çan quenjn quipoloa: uel quicocoltia, quellelaxitia, ça quen quimattoc, ça mopopoçauhtoc, ça içomocatoc, ça micqui in quioalmaiaui atenco: aiac uel ipan tlatoa, vncan quimonana in intahoan, in innahoan. Auh in aquin quitlamauhcaittilia, in quitlatẽmachilia ipiltzin, inic amo catlampapachozque: conquistiaia itlatzin quinmacaia in tlamacazque, aço totolin, aço tlaqualli: ic quicaoaia.

water, in order that they should let him go, he offered the priests something of value—either a turkey or food. In return for it they let [his son] be.

And when this came to pass, everywhere, in the houses of all, in each house, *etzalli*[9] was eaten. Each one made *etzalli* for himself; and there was a dance in which *etzalli* was begged. With green maize stalks they danced. Those who danced the *etzalli* dance entered house after house, each one begging and asking. [The householders] offered them all this same *etzalli,* [placing it] in the small jars, the *etzalli* jars, which they bore in their hands.

These [gods] were called Tlalocs. To them were attributed clouds, rain, hail, snow, mist, sheet lightning, thunder, and lightning bolts which struck men.

The Rainbow

As if arched—bent and rounded—it thus appeared. Varicolored, many-hued was its appearance. The single colors which showed in it [were] green, dark green, blue green, and black; and yellow and orange or tawny; then vermillion and ruby red; and [various shades of] blue, and dark green.[10]

And they said that when it appeared it revealed, made evident to men, and denoted—whereby it was known, realized, and seen—that it would not rain; would not rain hard—would not pour. But it would break up the clouds. It would dissipate, impede, and quiet the rain—the downpour which wet, soaked, and drenched one. If clouds piled up, if heavy clouds blackened [the sky] so that everywhere it was dark, it only dissipated [them]. Although it rained, no longer was the rain heavy; no longer did it increase. It only sprinkled; it drizzled; a few drops fell; a haze, a fog, a thin mist drifted and fell. Or at most it sprinkled; the sprinkling and the spray continued.

And they said—it was averred—[that] if it appeared over maguey plants, because of it the green [leaves] yellowed, turned, dried, reddened, and withered. And also they said [that] when it appeared many times, thereby it was evident [that] the rains were to end forthwith. They said: "Soon the masters of the rain will go; already the Tlalocs are about to leave."

Auh in icoac, y, in nouiian techachan, in cecencalpan etzalqualoia: ceceiaca metzalhuiaia, yoan etzalmaceoaloia: cintopiltica mitotia, tepan cacalaqui, motlatlaeuia, motlatlaitlanja, in etzalmaceuhque: çan muche in etzalli quinmaca, inxoxochuicol, imeetzalcon intlan caana.

In iehoantin, y, moteneoa tlaloque: intech tlamiloia in mistli, in quiauitl, in teciuitl, in cêpaiauitl, in aiauitl, in tlapetlaniliztli, in tlatlatziniliztli, in teuitequiliztli.

Aiauhcoçamalotl.

Iuhquin uitoliuhqui: tlauitoltic, coltic, inic oalmoquetza, tlatlatlapalpoalli, motlatlapalpouh in itlachieliz. In centlamantli tlapalli, itech neci: xoxoctic, quiltic, quilpaltic, iiapaltic, quilpalli, iiapalli: yoan coztic, xopaltic, xochipalli: niman ie chichiltic, tlapaltic: yoã tlaztaleoaltic, tlaztaleoalli: yoan texôtic, texôtli, matlaltic, matlalli.

Auh quitoa, in icoac oalmoquetza: quinestia, quiteittitia, quinezcaiotia, ic macho, ic machizti, ic itto: in amo quiauiz, amo tlaelquiauiz, amo tilaoaz: çan quimomoiaoaz in mistli, quipopoloa, quelleltia, quiiacatzacuilia in quiiauitl, in tlaelquiiauitl: in tepaltili, in techacoani, in teçoquitili. Intla cenca omotlatlali mistli, in ouel cuicuicheoac, in onouiian tlatlaiooac: çan quipopopoloa. Intlanel quiaui, aocmo cenca tilaoa, aocmo molhuia: ça aoachquiaui, aoachtli in onueuetzi, in onchichipini: aoachpitzactli, aoachpicilli, aoachpiciltoton, in ontzitzicuini in onueuetzi: anoçe çan aoachtilaoa, aoachtilaoatimani, aoachtzetzeliuhtimani.

Auh quitoa, quilmach intla metl, ipan moquetza: ic macueçaliciui, macoçauia, maoaqui, machichiliui, matlatlauja, macuetlauja. No yoan quitoa, in icoac miecpa oalmoquetza: ic neci, çan cuel quiçaz, in quiiauitl: quitoaia, çan cuel iazque in aoaque, ie quiçazque in tlaloque.

---

9. *Etzalli:* cf. Anderson and Dibble, *op. cit.,* II, p. 79.

10. Sahagún (*Memoriales con escolios*) has green for *xoxoctic, quiltic, quilpaltic, iiapaltic, quilpalli,* and *iiapalli.* Alonso de Molina, in his *Vocabulario de la lengua mexicana* (Julio Platzmann, ed.; Leipzig: B. G. Teubner, 1880), gives blue-green for *quilpaltic* and brown or black for *iiapaltic.* The second occurrence of this latter and of *quilpalli* is omitted in this translation. Molina translates *xochipaltic* as ruddy or rose-colored. In *Memoriales con escolios,* Sahagún treats both *chichiltic* and *tlapaltic* as red. For *tlaztaleoaltic,* Molina has red or rose-colored. For *matlaltic* and *matlalli,* the *Memoriales* has blue.

Sixth Chapter. Here are mentioned the snow, the clouds, and the hail.

[Frost]

The frost [god] was called Itztlacoliuhqui. Once yearly the cold came. During the feast of Ochpaniztli the cold began. And for one hundred and twenty days—one hundred and twenty suns—this persisted and there was cold. And it ended and disappeared [during the feast] called Tititl.

When [the month] came to an end, it was said: "For the frost hath departed. Now there will be sowing—it will be the time of sowing. Already land will be planted, so that [seeds] will be placed in the soil. Already it is warm, mild, calm. Already the season is good, the time is propitious; the hour is at hand; the time is ripe; the moment hath come." [For] already they hastened and were diligent. Already there was unrest; all men would be agitated and solicitous; they would be preoccupied. No longer would there be rest. Already the days would fly;[11] already there would be the setting forth for the working of the fields, the fresh working of the soil, the reworking of the fields; already the fields would be reworked. Now there would be planting of beans; beans would be placed. Now amaranth seed would be cast broadside; amaranth would be placed. Now *chía* seed would be cast; chili plants set out and transplanted. Already off-shoots would be pruned and separated, and all would bear fruit.

Snow

It was only the servant and companion which followed, accompanied, and spread the frost over the earth. It was considered to be like the rain. And it was said that when there was snow, [crops] would be harvested; the crops would be good. It foretold, and was an omen of, [good] crops.

Ic chicoacen capitulo, vncan mitoa: in cêpaiauitl, yoan mistli, yoan in teciuitl.

Cetl, mitoa: itztlacoliuhqui, cexiuhtica in oallatiuh, in ceuetzi: ipan ochpaniztli, in peoa ceuetzi. Auh chicoacempoalilhuitl, chiquacêpoaltonal: in mani, in ceuetzi. Auh ipan quiça, ipan poliui, in itoca tititl:

icoac tlami, mitoa ca oquiz in cetl, ie tocoz, ie toquizpan, ie tlatlalaquiloz, ic tlallan ontlatlaliloz: ie tlatotonja, ie tlacacaoaca, ie tlaiamanja: ie qualcan, ie uncan, ie inman, ie tlainman, otlainmantic: ie tlaciui, otlaciuh, ie neamaloz, ie neacomanaloz, ie nemociuiloz, ie tlamociuiz, aoc onnetlaliloz: ie tlacaitl eoaz, ie motocaz in tlaelimictli, in tlapopoxolli, in çacamolli, ie çacamoloz, ie etlaxoz, ie etlaçaloz: ie oauhpixoloz, ie oauhquetzaloz, ie chiempixoloz, ie chiltecoz, ie chilaquiloz: ie onpipilcotoz, ie onnemaiaohoaz, ie netlacatiloz.

Cepaiauitl,

Çan iuical, çan itlauical, quitoquilia, quitocatiuh, yoã onotiuh in cetl: iuhquin quiauitl ipan poui. Auh mitoa, in icoac cepaiaui: piscoz, tlamochioaz: quinestia, inezca in pisquiztli.

---

11. Here we follow Leonhard Schultze Jena: *Wahrsagerei, Himmelskunde und Kalender der alter Azteken, aus dem aztekischen Urtext Bernardino de Sahagún's übersetzt und erläutert* (Stuttgart: W. Kohlhammer Verlag, 1950), pp. 53, 368-369. An alternative, however, might be "men set forth, or arise" (*tlacatl, eua*).

Our rendition of *onpipilcotoz* and *onnemaiaohoaz* is provisional.

Clouds

When [clouds] billowed and formed thunderheads, settled, and hung [about the mountain tops], it was said: "The Tlalocs are already coming. Now it will rain. Now the masters of the rain will sprinkle water."

Hail

It was formed and took shape when very white clouds settled on mountain tops. It was said: "Now it will hail; now our food will be hailed out."

And thus did hail fall, making a din as of rattling, beating one about the head, pelting one [as if] with stones. Thus, truly, died and were despoiled our crops. For some distance, it flattened on the ground and spread birds over the surface of the water. At that time the water dwellers went gathering for themselves; they brought in their catch.

And that it might not hail, that they might not be hailed upon, and the young maize plants might not be damaged by hail, then the [sorcerers who] cast away hail and rain drove and headed it off. They removed it from the waters [of the lake]; they showed it the way and took it [hence]. Or else they cast it forth into the deserted places, the uncultivated lands where there were no crops, no one lived, and nothing existed; poverty-ridden lands—barren lands where nothing grew, nothing issued: the land was void. It was only an abandoned place; the [very] stones were dry.

Mistli.

In icoac tepeticpac moloni, momoloca, motlatlalia, mopiloa: mitoaia, ca ie uitze in tlaloque, ie quiiauiz, ie pixauizque in aoaque.

Teciuitl

Ic muchioa, ic neci: in icoac tepeticpac motlatlalia mistli, cẽca iztac: mitoa, ca ie teciuiz, ie teciuiloz in tonacaiotl.

Auh inic uetzi teciuitl, iuhquin tlacacalaca, tequacacalanja, temomotla: vel ic miqui, ic ispoliui, ic tonacamiqui, cematl quīmana, atlisco quinmana in totome. Auh vel oncan mopisquia, quin mopisquia, tonacatlama, in atlaca.

Auh inic amo teciuiz, inic amo teciuiloz, inic amo tecinmiquiz toctli: niman quitopeoa, quipeuia, in teciuhtlazque, in quiiiauhtlazque: atlanpa quiquanja, quitlachieltia, quiuica: anoço vmpa quitlaça in çacatla, çacaistlaoacan, in atle imuchioaian, atle iionoia, atle onoc, atle iieoaia, atle eoatoc, atle iquiçaiã, atle quiztoc, atle onuetztoc: çan iuhcatla, tetl oaoacca.

The Seventh Chapter telleth of the year counter and the year sign.

One Rabbit

It is said [that this was] the year sign and year counter of the south. For thirteen years it carried, set on its path, took with it, and bore the burden [of the years]. Always, during each [of the thirteen] years, it was the first, the one which led, began, became the start, and introduced as many year signs as there were: Reed, Flint, and House. Of the one [known as] Reed, it was said [that it was] as it were the sign of the east; that is, the year sign of the sun. For from there issued the light which shone forth.

And the third year sign, the one [known as] Flint, was called the sign of the north. For [the north] was said to be toward the land of the dead. Thus have the old people spoken: it is said that when one died, to that place set out, went straightway, and proceeded the dead. Therefore, when someone died—when [the sextons] adorned him, when they wrapped him in his mantle and bound him [in wrappings]—they made him look toward and seated him looking to that place.

And the fourth year sign, the fourth in order, [was] the one known as House—the sign of the west. For this reason they named it Ciuatlampa: it is said that there dwelt but women; none of us men were there.

These four year signs, year count[ers], as many times as they came to appear, [so many times] they came to be the beginning year signs.

When all the thirteen-year [periods]—all four of them—had concluded, ended, and finished, thus proceeding around, to give and leave their works from year to year, this [last] one came to, stopped at, jogged, knocked against, and ended at Thirteen House, the sign of the west. That is, now it approached [the end of its] thirteen years of labor.

And then One Rabbit came to settle itself as the sign of the south. When this occurred and it established itself and began its work, thus to bear a year

Inic chicome capitulo, itechpa tlatoa: in xiuhtlapoalli, in xiuhtonalli.

Ce tochtli.

moteneoa: uitztlampa xiuhtonalli, xiuhtlapoalli: matlacxiuitl omei tlauica, tlaotlatoctia, tlatqui, tlamama. In muchipa cecexiuhtica, vel tlaiacatia, tlaiacana, quipeoaltia, ipeuhca muchioa, quitzintia in izquitetl xiuhtonalli in acatl, in tecpatl, in calli. In iehoatl acatl, mitoa: tlapcopa tonalli, iuhquinma, q. n. tlauilcopa xiuhtonalli: ipãpa ca umpa oalneci in tlauilli, in tlanestia.

Auh inic ei xiuhtonalli, iehoatl in tecpatl: moteneoa mictlampa tonalli, ipampa in mjtoa mictlampa: iuh quitoaia in veuetque, quilmach in icoac micoa: vmpa itztiui, vmpa tlamelaoa, vmpa tlatotoca in mimicque. Iehica, in icoac aquin miquia, in oconchichiuhque, in oconquiquimiloque, in oconiilpique: vmpa quitlachialtiaia, vmpa quitztiltitimotlaliaia.

Auh inic naui, tlanauhcaiotia, xiuhtonalli: iehoatl in calli moteneoa, cioatlampa tonalli. Ipãpan iuh quitoaia, cioatlampa: quilmach, çan muchi cioa umpa onoque, aocaque toquichtin.

Inin nauhteme xiuhtonaltin, xiuhtlapoaltin: izquiteme ceceppa moquetztiui, tonalpeuhcaiome muchiuhtiuj.

Inic muchi matlatlacxiuitl omeei, quitlamja, conaxitia, quitzonquistia nauhteistin: inic tlaiaoalotiui, quimomacatiui, quimocauilitiui, intequiuh, cecexiuhtica: iehoatl itech onaci, itech õmocaoa, itech ontzopi, itech ontlatzotzona, ontlatzonquistia in matlactlomei calli, cioatlampa tonalli. q. n. ie ocaxiti in matlacxiuitl omei itequiuh.

Auh niman ic oalmoquetza in ce tochtli: uitztlampa tonalli. In icoac, y, moquetza, in quipeoaltia itequiuh, inic ce xiuitl tlauicaz, tlaotlatoctiz: cenca

and set it upon its way, all were much frightened and there was apprehension; all were filled with dread because in this [year] occurred the famine called Necetochuiliztli. All were exceedingly terrified and in awe when [the year] One Rabbit came—when they reached and came to it; though not [when it was] Two or Three [Rabbit]. Etc.

nemauhtiloia, tlatēmachoia, netēmachoa: ipampa, in ipan muchioaia maianaliztli, moteneoa necetochuiliztli. Çaniio uellamauhtiaia, uel imacaxoia: in icoac on omoquetz ce tochtli, in onoitech axioac, onoitech onpachiooac: amono ie in ome, anoço ey. etc.

The Eighth Chapter telleth how they held in dread hunger and famine when One Rabbit ruled the year count, and what they first did when the year count of One Rabbit had not yet begun.

And [even] when [the year] One Rabbit had not yet set in, first provision was made; our food was hidden away, stored, saved up, and placed in bins. Nothing was thrown away; all then was saved—wild seeds not commonly eaten; musty maize; corn silk; corn tassels; pulp scraped from maguey tappings, tuna cactus flowers; cooked maguey leaves; heated maguey sap.

Everything was taken into account: [with] amaranth, even the weeds[12] were threshed; [as for] the beans, likewise were stored and put away unripened ones and the dried, withered ends of the green beans. and when they had used all, they satisfied and quickened themselves [with] bird seed, bitter amaranth or bright red amaranth, and *yacacolli* maize.[13]

This was the time when they bought people;[14] they purchased men for themselves. The merchants were those who had plenty, who prospered; the greedy, the well-fed man, the covetous, the niggardly, the miser, who controlled wealth and family, guardians, the mean, the stingy, the selfish. In the homes of [such men] they crowded, going into bondage, entering house after house—the orphan, the poor, the indigent, the needy, the pauper, the beggar, who were starved and famished; who just as they went to sleep, just so awoke; who found nothing and got nowhere; who in no place found their rest, relief or remedy. At this time one sold oneself. One ate oneself; one swallowed oneself. Or else one sold and delivered into bondage his beloved son, his dear child.

Inic chicuey capitulo, itechpa tlatoa: inic quimacacia apiztli, in maianaliztli, in icoac tlauicaia, in xiuhtlapoalli in ce tochtli: yoan in tlein achtopa quichioaia, in aiamo vmpeoa xiuhtlapoalli, ce tochtli.

Auh in icoac, aiamo moquetza ce tochtli: achtopa nenemachtiloia, netlatlatililo, netetzontilo, netacatilo, mocuezcomatema in tonacaiotl: aoc tle motlaça, muchicoac netlatililo in polocatl, in popoiotl, in xilotzõtli, in miiaoatl, in metzolli, in nochxochitl, in mescalli, in necutlatotonilli.

Auh inic muchi temachiloia, in oauhtli çan yoã mosconoa in ipolocaio: in etl çan yoan motlatiaia, mocalaquiaia in iaxaoacaio, yoan in jexococoloio in opatzaoac. Auh icoac, muchi tlaiecoa, tlaacotlaça tlaihiiocuitia in petzicatl, in chichic oauhtli, anoço teuoauhtli, iacacolli:

ie icoac tecoa, motlacacouia, in vnca quicoani, in mocuiltonoa, in motlacamati, in tlâtlametl, tlaisxotiani, atle quiscaoa, tlaistamachiuhqui, tlaçaloani, tlapachoani, tlamalhuiani, teuie, tzotzoca, motzol: ichan maaquia, mihioa, mocacalaquia in icnotlacatl, in motolinja, in quiciaui, in quihiiouia: in aoneoatinemi, in aonmacitinemi, in apizmicqui, in teuciuhque: in iuhqui cochi, in iuhqui meoa, in aualnecini, in aoccan vitz, in aoccan quitta ihiiocuiia, iceuhca, ipatica: ie vncan in monamaca, in moqua, in motoloa: anoço quinamaca, quimonamaquilia in ipiltzin, in iconetzin:

---

12. *In oauhtli çan yoã in ipolocaio:* cf. Bernardino de Sahagún: *Historia general de las cosas de Nueva España* (México: Editorial Pedro Robredo, 1938), II, p. 268: "huauhtli polocayo, *es la semilla de los cenizos sin limpiar, con todas sus inmundicias.*" Jena, *op. cit.,* p. 69. has "*körnte man sogar auch die Beermelde aus.*"

13. Some of these terms are identified in Anderson and Dibble, *op. cit.,* II, p. 63. *Yacacolli* is described in Bernardino de Sahagún: *Histoire générale des choses de la Nouvelle-Espagne* (D. Jourdanet and Rémi Siméon, eds.; Paris: G. Masson, Editeur, 1880), p. 118, n. 2, as "*espèce de maïs.*" See also the Robredo edition, Vol. I, p. 159.

14. The translation of this passage differs in some details from that of Jena (*op. cit.,* pp. 68-71), *q. v.*

Quicoani appears in the *Real Palacio MS* as *quiquani.* The term could be translated, "those who ate people." Cf. *in moqua* (one ate oneself), toward the end of the paragraph.

[For] they had incurred sins. They had taken unto themselves, and placed themselves in, great wrong, through which they went always being slaves, until at last they were to die.

And even if he died, once again some one of his kin stood surety for him. Or else his beloved son offered himself and finished for him. None were neglected. Their kin and their lineage went on continuing and extending [the obligation]; they went on paying the debt and concerning themselves [with it]. Always they fulfilled the pledge, continued taking the place of others, served for one another; they all entered the households of their lords.

If sons or grandsons were born to him, at once [their elders] assigned them their great faults. When they matured, when they gained prudence, when they looked about, already servitude would be upon them. Already they wielded the hoe, they used the tump line; already they were [as] someone else's dogs, someone else's turkeys. For in truth [slavery] had come upon them; they had come against that which they could not leave—of which they could not be rid. For their fathers, their grandfathers, their mothers, and their grandmothers had proceeded to merit for them, to acknowledge for them, to bequeath them, to load and place upon them, [their transgressions]. For difficult was that which they had left and bequeathed them in time of famine—those who hungered and starved, who no longer were proud, who no longer persevered, who indeed were sick; who had eaten themselves, had sold themselves.

[This was] because they had prepared nothing for themselves, had shown no forethought for themselves; had paid no heed, had lived in negligence, and were disposed to evil before the year sign One Rabbit had begun—[when] it had not yet set in.

Thus was it said, that their fathers and grandfathers had succumbed to One Rabbit; hence they took on great sins.

When [the year] One Rabbit had fulfilled its task, when the year had been completed, then it delivered its charge to the sign of the east: Two Reed was the one which [then] set in.

motlatlaculnamictia, ueuetlatlaculli quimottitia, quimotlalilia: inic muchipa centlacotli ietiuh, in isquich cauitl miquiz.

Auh in manel onmic, oc ceppa ipan oalmoquetza, aca ioaniolqui, anoço ipiltzin õmisquetza, ipan tlaiecoa: aiac miscaoa, ma antiui, motilinitiui, cemololiuhtiui, mocemichictiui in incalloc, in incuitlaxcolloc: muchipa impan tlaiecoa, impan oonotiui, mocepanpaleuia, cencalaqui in ichan intecuiio:

intla tlacatizque ipilhoan, in imisuioan, çan niman ie quincauilitiui in inueuetlacol: in oalmozcalizque, in oalistlamatizque, in oallachiazque, ie intech ca in intlacoio, ie uicti, ie mecapalti, ie teitzcuinhoan, ie tetotolhoan: ca nel oimpan ia, oquimonamictique, in auel tecauh, in auel poliui: ca intahoã, inculhoan, innanhoã, incihoã in quinmaceuitiui, quincuititiui, quincauilitiui, quinmamaltitiui, quintlalilitiui: ca ouicã in concauhque, in quimoncauilique, inic maianalco, in teuciuiian, im apizmiquia, aoc imatlamatia, aoc ontlaiecoa, uel icocoiaia: in moquaque, in monamacaque.

Ipampa, in atle cõmochioaltique, in atle ic onmotlamachique, in aquen ommomatque, in çan onmotlacomatque, onmauilmatque: in icoac aiamo peoa, aiamo moquetza xiuhtonalli ce tochtli.

Ic mitoa, ca mocetochuique in intahoan in inculhoan: inic quicuique veuetlatlacolli.

In icoac, ie otequit ce tochtli, in otlatzonquisti ce xiuitl: niman ic ie itech concaoa, in tlapcopa tonalli: iehoatl oalmoquetza in vme acatl.

Ninth Chapter, in which is described what was called "The Binding of Our Years," or "When the Years are Bound," [which occurred] when one by one the four year signs had each reigned thirteen years and when fifty-two years had passed; and what then was done.

When [came] the time of the binding of our years, always they gradually neared and approached [the year] Two Reed. This is to say: they then reached and ended [a period of] fifty-two years. For at that time [these years] were piled up, added one to another, and brought together; wherefore the thirteen-year [cycles] had four times made a circle,[15] as hath been made known. Hence was it said that then were tied and bound our years, and that once again the years were newly laid hold of. When it was evident that the years lay ready to burst into life, everyone took hold of them, so that once more would start forth—once again—another [period of] fifty-two years. Then [the two cycles] might proceed to reach one hundred and four years. It was called "One Old Age" when twice they had made the round, when twice the times of binding the years had come together.

Behold what was done when the years were bound —when was reached the time when they were to draw the new fire,[16] when now its count was accomplished. First they put out fires everywhere in the country round. And the statues, hewn in either wood or stone, kept in each man's home and regarded as gods, were all cast into the water. Also [were] these [cast away]—the pestles and the [three] hearth stones [upon which the cooking pots rested]; and everywhere there was much sweeping—there was sweeping very clean. Rubbish was thrown out; none lay in any of the houses.

And when they drew the new fire, they drew it there at Uixachtlan, at midnight, when the night divided in half. They drew it upon the breast of a

Inic chicunaui capitulo, vncan mitoa: in mitoa, toximmolpili, anoço inic molpilia xiuitl: yn icoac matlatlacpa omeexpa otlauicac, yn inauhteixti cecentetl xippoalli: inic onaci vmpoalxiuitl ipan matlacxiuitl omume, yoan in tlein icoac muchioaya.

Ie vncan, ie ipan in toxiuhmolpilia: muchipa ie quimattiuh, quitztiuh in vme acatl. q. n. Ca vncan aci, uncan tlami ompoalxiuitl õmatlactli, yoã onxiuitl. Ca vncan mocentlalia, monepanoa, monamiqui: inic otlaiaoalo nauhcampa matlacxiuitl omeey, in iuh omoteneuh: ic mitoa, vncan molpia, molpilia in toxiuh, oc ceppa iancuican vncan xiuhtzitzquilo: inic monezcaiotiaia, in xiuitl isoatoc, muchi tlacatl cõquitzquiaia, inic oc ceppa ie õpeoa, oc no izqui xiuitl 52 años, inic acitiuh macuilpoalxiuitl ipan nauhxiuitl: mitoa cen ueuetiliztli, in oppa tlaiaoaloa, in oppa monamiqui imolpilican xiuitl.

Izcatqui in muchioaia, icoac molpilia xiuitl: in icoac oaxioac, in vncã uetziz tlequauitl, in ie itlapoalpan: achto vel nouiian cêceuia in tletl in cematonaoac, yoan in isquich pieloia techachã, in neteutiloia tequacuilti, in aço quauitl, anoço tetl tlaxintli, muchi atlan onmotepeoaia: No iehoatl in texolotl, in tenamaztli, yoan nouiian tlâtlachpanoia, tlatetzcalolo, tlanaoac tlauico, aoctle uetztoia in techachan.

Auh in vetzia tlequauitl, vmpa in vixachtlan: iooalnepantla in vetzia, vel icoac in xeliui iooalli: malli in ielpan vetzia, iehoatl in tlaçopilli ielpan in quimama-

15. See Plate 20.

16. *uetziz tlequauitl:* literally, "the fire stick will fall." The obvious meaning and the grammatical structure are not in agreement and we have adopted the obvious meaning in our translations of the phrase.

captive, and it was a well-born one on whose breast [the priest] bored the fire drill. And when a little [fire] fell, when it took flame, then speedily [the priest] slashed open the breast of the captive, seized his heart, and quickly cast it there into the fire. Thus he fed, he served it to the fire. And the body of [the captive] all came to an end in the flames. And those who drew fire were exclusively the priests, the fire priests, the devout. Of the fire priest of Copulco, who was experienced, it was his office to draw, to drill, the new fire.

lia tlequauitl. Auh in icoac quẽteltzin ouetz, in omopitz: niman ic iciuhca, queltetectiuetzi in malli, conanjlia in iiollo, tleco contlaztiuetzi: inic quicoaltia, quitlamaca tletl. Auh in inacaio, çan muchi tleco tlami. Auh in tlequauhtlaçaia, çan iehoã in tlamacazque, in tlenamacaque, in tlamaceuhque: copolco tlenamacac, in vel imatia, in itequiuh catca, in quitlaçaia, in quimamalia tlequauitl.

Tenth Chapter, wherein is described the disposition of those who kept watch when the new fire appeared.

At nightfall, from here in Mexico, they departed. All the fire priests were arranged in order, arrayed in and wearing the garb of the gods. Each one represented and was the likeness of perhaps Quetzalcoatl, or Tlaloc, etc., or whichever one he went representing. Very deliberately, very stately, they proceeded, went spread out, and slowly moved. It was said: "They walk like gods." Thus, in deep night, they arrived there at Uixachtlan.

And the one who was the fire priest of Copulco, who drew new fire, then began there. With his hands he proceeded to bore continuously his fire drill; he went about making trials with his drill, the fire-maker.

And when it came to pass that night fell, all were frightened and filled with dread. Thus was it said: it was claimed that if fire could not be drawn, then [the sun] would be destroyed forever; all would be ended; there would evermore be night. Nevermore would the sun come forth. Night would prevail forever, and the demons of darkness would descend, to eat men.

Hence everyone ascended the terraces; all went upon the housetops. No one was on the ground below. The house was abandoned. They sat. And women with child put on masks of maguey leaves and took up their maguey-leaf masks. And [they] placed [the women] in granaries, for they were looked upon with fear. It was said and claimed that if, truly, the new fire were not drawn, these also would eat men; [for] they would be changed into fierce beasts.

And the small children they likewise masked with maguey leaves. None [of them] could sleep, or close, shut, or [even] half-close their eyes. From time to time their mothers and fathers were [there with them]; they kept waking them, punching and nudging them, calling out to them. They woke, cuffed, and nudged them. Because if they were to

Inic matlactli capitulo, vncan moteneoa, in tlatecpaniliztli: in quipiaia, inic iãcuic tletl necia.

Ie tlapoiaoa, in nican oneoaia mexico: motecpantiuia muchinti in tletlenamacaque, muchichiuhtiui, ommaaquia in intlatqui teteu: in ceceniaca impan mixeoaia, quinmixiptlatiaia, in aço quetzalcoatl, anoço tlaloc et^a in çaço ac iehoatl ipan quiztiuia, cenca çan iiolic, cenca çan iuian in iatiuiia, onotiuiia, mantiuiia: moteneoa, teunenemi, inic uellaquauhiooa onaci, vmpa uixachtlã.

Auh in iehoatl copolco tlenamacac, in tlequauhtlazqui: niman nican quipeoaltia, in imac quimamamaltiuh itlequauh: quiiehecotiuh ica in imamalioaca, in itlaçaloca.

In iqoac, y, oiooac, cenca nemauhtiloia, tlatenmachoia: iuh mitoaia, quilmach intlacamo, uel vetziz tlequauitl: vncan cempoliooaz, centlamoaz, centlaiooaz, aocmo oalquiçaz in tonatiuh: ie ic centlaiooa, oaltemozque in tzitzitzimi, tequaquiui:

ic muchi tlacatl itlapanco tlecoia, netlapantemaloia, aocac tlalchi, tlatzintla, cali mocaoaia, motlaliaia. Auh in ootzti, momexaiacatiaia, inmemexaiac quicuia, yoan cuezcomac quintlaliaia: ipampa mauhcaittoia, iuh mitoaia, quilmach intlaca uel uetzi tlequauitl: no iehoantin tequazque, motequãcuepazque.

Auh in pipiltotõti, no quinmemexaiacatiaia: aiac vel oncochia, onicopia, onmispiquia, onjsmotzoloaia: çan ic cate in innãhoan, in intahoã, quimixititicate, quintipiniticate, quintiloticate, quintzatzatzatziliticate, quimixitia, quintipinja, quintiloa: ipampa intla oncochizque, quilmach quiquimichtin mocuepazque, quimichtizque.

sleep—it was thought—they would turn into mice; they would become mice.

Hence was heed paid only one thing; there was unwavering attention and expectation as all remained facing, with neck craned, the summit of Uixachtecatl. Everyone was apprehensive, waiting until, in time, the new fire might be drawn—until, in good time, [a flame] would burst forth and shine out. And when a little came forth, when it took fire, lit, and blazed, then it flared and burst into flames, and was visible everywhere. It was seen from afar.

Then all the people quickly cut their ears, and spattered the blood repeatedly toward the fire. Although [a child] still lay in the cradle, they also cut his ears, took his blood, and spattered it [toward] the fire. Thus, it was said, everyone performed a penance.

Then [the priests] slashed open [the captive's] breast. In his breast [cavity] the new fire was drawn. They opened the breast of the captive with a flint knife called *ixquauac*. Etc.

Ic ça miscauja, mocemmati in ontlachielotoc, in onitztotoc, in õnequechanotoc, uixachtecatl iicpac: isquich tlacatl vmpa ontlatenmati, õmotemachia, in quẽmanja uetzi tlequauitl, in quẽmania oalcueponi, oalpetzini. Auh in icoac, oquenteltzin vel uetz, in omopitz, in oxotlac: çatepan ic cuetlani, cueponi, nouiian õneci, oalitto in vêca.

Niman ic muchi tlacatl monacaztectiuetzi, contlatzitzicuinilia ixquichcapa in tletl: in manel coçolco onoc no connacaztequi, concuilia iniezço, contzitzicuinilia in tletl: ic mitoa, ca muchi tlacatl tlamaceoa,

ic coneltetequi, in jelpan ontlequauhtlaxoc, conelcoionja in malli, ica tecpatl: itoca isquaoac. etc.[a]

28

Eleventh Chapter, in which is told what they did when it was seen and was evident that the new fire burst out.

And then everyone—the priests and fire priests—took the fire from there. [Having come] from all directions, the fire priests of Mexico had been sent there, charged with the task, as well as those who had come from distant [places] everywhere—messengers and runners. For these were all only chosen ones, strong warriors, valiant men, picked as best; the fleet, the swift, who could run like the wind. Because through them they could quickly have fire come to their cities.

First, the fire brand was prepared and adorned. It was called *tlepilli*. And this the fire priests brought. Before [doing] anything else, they took it up, direct, to the top of the temple [pyramid], where was kept the image of Uitzilopochtli, and placed it in the fire holder.[17] Then they scattered and strewed white incense [over it]. And then they came down, and, also before [doing] anything further, they brought and took it direct to the priests' house, the place named Mexico.[18] Later, this was dispersed, and fires were started everywhere in each priests' house and each calpulli; whereupon it went everywhere to each of the young men's houses. At that time all of the common folk came to the flame, hurled themselves at it, and blistered themselves as fire was taken. When thus the fire had been quickly distributed everywhere among them, there was the laying of many fires; there was the quieting of many hearts.

This same all the village fire priests did. That is, they carried the fire and made it hasten. Much did they goad [the runners] and make them hurry, so that they might speedily bring it to their homes. They hurried to give it to one another and take it from one another; in this way they went alternating with one another. Without delay, with ease, in a

Inic matlactloce capitulo, vncan mitoa: in tlein quichioaia, in icoac omottac, onez, in ocuepon iãcuic tletl.

Auh quinicoac, isquich tlacatl vmpa tlecui, in tlamacazque, in tletlenamacaque: inic ie nouiiampa vmpa oioaloque, oisquetzaloque, in mexico tlenamacaque, yoan in ie nouiian veca oaleoa, titlanti, tlaioaltin: ca çan much iehoan in pepenaloia, chicaoaque, in oquichtin, in tiacaoan in tlatzonanti, in painanj, in tlacçani, in iuhqui hecatoca ic motlaloa: ipampa inic iciuhca, caxititiuetzizque tletl imaltepeuh ipan:

ca achtopa ic nenemachtiloia, muchichioaia in tlecuioani: itoca tlepilli. Auh ieehoatl, ic quioalaxitiaia in tlenamacaque: oc ie achto, vmpa quitlecauiaia, quitlamelaoaltiaia in iicpac teucalli: in vmpa mopieia ixiptla vitzilobuchtli, tlequazco contlaliaia: nimã ic contepeoa, contoxaoa in iztac copalli. Auh niman ic oaltemo, oc ie no achto, vmpa quitqui, quitlamelaualtia in calmecac, itocaiocã mexico: ic çatepan moiaoa, tletletlalilo in nouiian cacalmecac, cacalpulco: niman ie ic iauh, in nouiian tetelpuchcalli. Ie vncan in isquich onxoquiui, onmotepeoa, ontapaliui maceoalli, in motlecuilia: icoac ic nouiian, tepan moiaoatiuetzi in tletl netletletlalilolo, neioiollalilo.

Çã no iuh quichioa, in isquich altepeoa tlenamacac: inic quitquia, quinenemitiaia tletl, cẽca quitototzaia, quimotlalochtiaia: inic iciuhca caxitizque inchan, quimomamacatiquiça, quimocuicuilitiquiça: ic mopapatlatiui. Amo uecauh, amo machiztli, çan isquich cauitl, y, in conaxitiaia, in quicueponaltiaia: çan achitonca in nouiiampa, cuecuepocatimoteca

---

17. "*Vn candelero, hecho de cal y canto, puesto delante del ydolo*"—corresponding Spanish text.

18. Sahagún, in the corresponding Spanish text, thus explains this distribution: "*I de alli tomauã y lleuauan al aposento de los sacerdotes, que se dizẽ mexicanos: y despues a otros aposentos, de los dichos mjnistros, de ydolos: y de alli tomauan, y lleuauan todos yos vezinos, de la ciudad.*"

short time they caused it to come and made it flare up. In a short time everywhere fires burst forth and flared up quickly. Also there they first carried and brought it direct to their temples, their priests' houses, and each of their calpullis. Later it was divided and spread among all everywhere in each neighborhood and in the houses.

tletl, cuecuepocatiquiça: no vmpa achto quitquitiquiça, quitlamelaoaltitiuetzi in inteupan, in incalmecac, in incacalpulco: çatepan ic moiaoa, tepan cẽmani in nouiian tlâtlaxilacalpan, yoan in calpan.

Twelfth Chapter, in which is told [the manner of conduct of] all the people when the new fire was taken. And, when this took place, everyone renewed his clothing and all the household goods.

Then, at this time, all renewed their household goods, the men's array, and the women's array, the mats—the mats of large, fat reeds,—and the seats. All was new which was spread about, as well as the hearth stones and the pestles. Also at this time [the men] were newly dressed and wrapped in capes. A woman—[such as she] dressed newly in their new skirts and shifts.

Thus it was said that truly the year newly started. There was much happiness and rejoicing. And they said: "For thus it is ended; thus sickness and famine have left us." Then incense was offered; [quail] were decapitated, and incense was offered. They grasped this incense ladle, and raised it in dedication to the four directions in the courtyard. Then they cast it into the hearth. Thus was incense offered.

Thereupon amaranth seed cakes overspread with honey were eaten. Then all were bidden to fast, and [it was ordered] that no one should drink from the time that it was completely light until it came to be considered midday. And when noon came, then captives and ceremonially bathed ones died. Then all rejoiced and there was feasting. Then once again fires were newly laid and placed.

And [as for] the pregnant women who had been feared, if any of them then gave birth to and bore a child; if a boy was born as her child, they named him Molpilli, Xuihtlalpil, Xiuhtzitzqui, Xiuhtli, Texiuh, Xiuhtlatlac, Quetzalxiuh, Xiuhquen, etc. And if [it was] a girl, Xiuhnenetl, Xiuhcue, Xiuhcoçol, etc.

And when, in the time of Moctezuma, our years were bound, he ordered that indeed everywhere should be sought a captive whose name [contained the word] *xiuitl*. Wheresoever [he was], this one was to be seized. And one was taken—a man from Uexotzinco, a well-born man. He was called Xiuhtlamin,

Inic matlactlomume, capitulo, vncan mitoa: in quenin in isquich tlacatl, in icoac omocuic in iancuic tletl: auh in icoac, y, muchi tlacatl, quiiãcuiliaia in itlaquen, yoan in isquich calitlatquitl.

Niman icoac, isquich iancuiia, in calitlatquitl: in oquichtlatquitl, in cioatlatquitl, in petlatl, in tolcuestli, in icpalli: muchi iancuic in moteteca, ioã in tenamaztli, in texolotl. No iquac iancuic nequentilo, nelpililo in tilmatli: in cioatl, iancuic ommaquia, in incue, in inuipil.

Ic mitoa, ca nel iancuic onpeoa in xiuitl: papacoa, netlamachtilo: yoan quitoaia, ca ic oquiz, ic otechtlalcaui in cocoliztli, in maianaliztli. Niman ic cocopaltemalo, tlacotonalo, tlenamaco: concui in tlemaitl, nauhcampa coniiaoa in ithoalco, çatepan contema tlexicco, inic otlenamacoc copalli:

nimã ie ic necpan tzotzooalqualo, vncan ic neçaoaliztlalhuilo, inic aiac atliz, ic centlathuiz: quincenmomattiuiia in nepantla tonatiuh. Auh in oacic, nepantla tonatiuh, niman ic miqui in mamalti, yoan tlaaltilti: quinicoac cenpapacoa, tlâtlaqualo: icoac oc ceppa iãcuican netlêtlecuiltilo, netlêtlecuillalililo.

Auh in oimacaxoia ootzti, intla aca icoac omixiuh, otlacachiuh: intla oquichtli iconeuh otlacat, quitocaiotiaia molpili, xiuhtlalpil, xiuhtzitzqui, xiuhtli, texiuh, xiuhtlatlac, quetzalxiuh, xiuhquen. Etc.[a] Auh intla cioatl, xiuhnenetl, xiuhcue, xiuhcoçol. Etc.[a]

Auh in icoac, ipan muchiuh motecuçoma, toxiuhmolpili cenca nouiian ic tlanaoati, inic temoloz malli: in itoca xiuitl, in çaço campa iê anoz. Auh ce axioac uexotzincatl, tlaçopilli: itoca xiuhtlamin, tlatilulco malli muchiuh: in tlamanj itoca itzcuin, auh ic tocaiotiloc, ic notzaloc xiuhtlaminmani: ca iehoatl

and became a captive at Tlatilulco. The captor was named Itzcuin, and henceforth he was known as and called "Captor of Xiuhtlamin."[19] For on the breast of his captive fire was drawn by the drill, and all his body was consumed in the fire. And they made [the victim's] image of pure amaranth seed dough, so that it might represent him; they set cooked grains of maize upon it, so that they could give it to the people to eat.

ielpan uetz, in tlequauitl imal, muchi tleco tlan in jnacaio: auh ça tzohoalli, inic quixiptlaioti, in ipan quipouh: tlaolpaoastli ipan quitlatlali, inic quitequalti.

---

19. In the corresponding Spanish text, Sahagún writes: *"fue tomado un hombre de vexocingo, muy generoso: el qual se dezia, xiuhtlamjn: y lo tomo en la guerra, vn soldado de tlatilulco, que auja nõbre itzcujn: por lo qual despues, le llamauan a el, xiuhtlamjnmanj. . . ."* In Jena, op. cit., p. 79, the passage is translated: *"Und einer kam an einen Mann aus Vexotzinco, einen Mann vornehmer Abkunft, Xiuhtlamin mit Namen, aus Tlatilulco, den zum Kriegsgefangenen der Häscher machte, der Itzcuin hiess und der dementspechend der Namen erhielt und Xiuhtlaminmani genannt wurde."*

APPENDIX

De la manera que esta
este quaderno a de ir
toda la obra.—Saha-
gún, *Memoriales con
Escolios*

THE SEVENTH BOOK TREATETH OF THE SUN, MOON, AND STARS, AND OF THE YEAR OF JUBILEE

EL 7.º LIBRO TRATA DEL SOL Y DE LUNA Y ESTRELLAS Y DEL AÑO DEL JUBILEO.[20]

First Chapter, of the sun.

The sun hath the quality of shining and of lighting and of casting rays from himself. He is hot and he seareth; he maketh one sweat, and turneth a man's body and face dark brown or tawny.

El sol tiene propriedad de resplandecer y de alumbrar y de echar rayos de si. Es caliente y tuesta, haze sudar pa hosco o loro el cuerpo y la cara de la persona.

They celebrated a feast to the sun once each year in the sign named Four Olin. And before the feast they fasted four days as the vigil of the feast. And in this feast of the sun, four times they offered incense and blood from the ears—once at sunrise, another time at midday, at the vesper hour, and when [the sun had] set.

Hazian fiesta al sol vna vez cada año en el signo que se llama 4. olin. Y antes de la fiesta ayunavan quatro dias como vigilia de la fiesta. Y en esta fiesta del sol ofrecian encienso y sãgre de las orejas quatro vezes: vna en saliendo el sol, otra al medio dia, y a la hora de visperas y qñ se ponia.

Ytzcaliui. t. itzcaliuhtica in noyollo: My heart is calmed, or resteth, in love. Pret., oitzcaliuh. oitzcaliuhticatca.

33.
ytzcaliui. t. itzcaliuhtica yn noyollo. refriarse o declino mi coraçon en el amor. p̃t.º oitzcaliuh. oitzcaliuhticatca.

Vel cen tecomatl in atl ocontzineuh: A whole gourd[ful of water] was overturned while being drunk.

34.
Vel cen tecomatl ỹ atl ocontzineuh. trastornose vna xicara ẽtera beuiẽdola.

20. Sahagún (Paso y Troncoso ed.), Vol. VI, pp. 177-215.

INIC CHICOME AMUXTLI YTECHPA TLA-TOA YN TONATIUH, YOAN Ỹ METZTLI YOAN Ỹ CICITLALTI YOAN Ỹ TOXIM-MOLPIA

1.

Tonatiuh.

quauhtlevanitl. xippilli. teutl.
2.   3.   4.   5.   6.
Tona. tlanextia. motonameyotia. totonqui. tetlati.
　.7.   8.
tetlatlati. teytoni. teixtlileuh. teixtlilo. teixcaputzo.
　9.
teixtlecaleuh.

10.   11.
Matlacpoaltica ipan epoalli yn ilhuiuh quiçaya, yn
                        12.   13.
ilhuichiuililoya. ylhuiquixtililoya ypan quimattiuiya
      14.   15.
yn itonal ytoca naolin. Auh yn ayamo quiça ylhuiuh
16.   17. 18.   19.   20.   21.
achtopa navilhuitl neçaualoya. Auh yn iquac ye ipan
                22.   23.
ylhuiuh, yn iquac yancuicã valquiça. valmomana.
24.   25.   26.   27.
valpetzini: tlenamacoya. tlatotonilo. neçoa. Jn hin
28.   29.   30.   31.
muchiuaya nappa cemilhuitl: yquac in youatzinco,
32.   33.
yoan nepãtla tonatiuh, yoan yquac in ye õmotzcaloa,
                    34.
in ye õmopiloa: yoan iquac yn oncalaqui, yn onaqui,
                    35.
yn õmotzineua. Auh in youatzinco mitoaya, ca ye
36   37.   38. 39.
tequitiz, ye tlacotiz. yn tonatiuh quen vetziz ỹ cemil-
                    40.
huitl. Auh yn oyouac, mitoaya oteq't otlacotic yn
                41.   42.   43.
tonatiuh. Ynic valmomana yn quẽman vel eztic,
44.   45.   46.
chichiltic, tlapaltic. Auh yn quẽman çan yztalectic,

Capitulo Primero del Sol

1.

Sol

2.   3.
Resplandecer. p̃t.º otonac. alumbrar. p̃t.º otlanexti.
4.   5.
echar de si rayos. p̃t.º omotonameyoti. cosa caliente.
6.   7.   8.
cosa que tuesta. cosa que haze sudar. cosa que
                    9.
ẽnegreçe o para loro. leuanta los cueros tostandolos.

10.   11.
Cada dozientos y sesenta dias. hazer fiesta. p̃t.º
                    12.   13.   14.
onilhuichiuh. onilhuiquixti. en. seguirse. su signo.
                15.   16. 17. 18.
caso. notonal. nõbre. caso. notoca. antes. quatro dia.
                19.   20. 21.   22.
o fiesta. ayunar. p̃t.º oninoçauh. Y quando. p̃mera-
                    23.   24.
mente. Salir. p̃t.º oniquiz. oninoman. asomar. p̃t.º
                    25.
onipetzin. echar encienso cõ la mano de barro en que
                                26.
estan brasas. p̃t.º onitlenamacac. onitlatotoni. Vntarse
                                    27.
cõ sagre de las oreias las maxillas p̃t.º oniniçoc. Esto
                28.   29.   30.
se hazia. p̃t.º onicchiuh. quatro uezes. en vn dia.
31.   32.   33.
de mañana. al medio dia. pasar el sol de medio dia.
                    34.
p̃t.º õmotzcalo: õmopilo. Entrarse. p̃t.º ocalac. onac.
                35.   36.
õmotzineuh. Dezir algo. p̃t.º oniquito. trabaiar hazer
                    37.
tarea o destaxo. p̃t.º oniteq't. lo mismo. p̃t.º onitlacotic.
38.   39.   40.
de que manera. acontecer algo. p̃t.º ouetz. hazerse

And when he came forth in the morning, they said: "Now the sun starteth his work. How will it be? What will come to pass on this day?"

And at sunset they said: "The sun hath ended his work, or task." Sometimes when the sun riseth, he seemeth blood-colored; and at times whitish; and sometimes he riseth sickly-hued because of the mist or the clouds which cover him.

When the sun is eclipsed, he turneth red; it seemeth that the sun becometh disquieted, or troubled; or he moveth to and fro, or he stirreth. And he turneth very yellow.

When the people see this, they then raise a tumult.

And a great fear taketh them, and then the women weep aloud. And the men cry out, [at the same time] striking their mouths with [the palms of] their hands. And everywhere great shouts and cries and howls were raised. And then they hunted out men of fair hair and white faces; and they sacrificed them to the sun. And also they sacrificed captives, and they anointed themselves with the blood of their [own] ears. And, besides, they bored [the lobes of]

Y quando a la mañana salia dezian ya comiença el sol su obra que sera, que acontecera ẽ este dia.

Y a la puesta del sol, dezian acabo su obra, o su tarea el sol. A las vezes qñ sale el sol pareçe de color de sangre: y a las vezes parece blanquezino: y a las vezes sale de color enfermizo por razon de las nieblas o de las nubes que se le añponẽ.

Quando se eclipsa el sol parase colorado parece que se desasosiega o se turba el sol, o se remeçe, o rebuelue y amarillecese mucho.

Quando esto vee la gente luego se alborota.

Y tomales gran temor, y luego las mugeres lloran a vozes. Y los hombres dan grita hiriendo las bocas con la mano. Y en todas ptes se dauã grandes bozes y gritos, y alaridos. Y luego buscavan los hombres de cabellos blancos y caras blãcas: y los sacrificauan al sol. Y tambien sacrificauan captiuos y se vntauã con la sangre de las oreias: y tambien aguierauan las oreias con puntas de maguei y pasauan mimbres o cosa semeiante por los aguieros q̃ las puntas avian

47.   48.   49.   50.

çan camaztac, çan cocuxtiuh ypampa ỹ mixtli, ỹ

51.   52.   53.   54.

mixayauitl, anoço mixpanitl, mixtecuicuilli. yn ixco

55.

moteca.—

41.   42.

noche. p̃t.° oyouac. Presentarse a nosotros el sol. a las

43.   44.

vezes cosa de color de sangre. cosa colorada. lo

45.

mismo. Caso. nochichilticauh. notlapalticauh.

46.   47.

cosa blanquezina. caso noztalecticauh. la cara blan-

48.

quezina. Caso nocamaztacauh. echa claridad mor-

49.   50.

tezina. p̃t.° ocucuxtia. por razõ. de nubes. caso. nomix.

51.   52.

Nube como niebla. ca. nomixayauh. Vandera de

53.

nube. ca. nomixpan. Nubes de diuersas colores ca.

54.   55.

nomixtecuicuil. delante la cara. ca. nixco. ponerse

algo o echarse. p̃t.° omotecac.

1.

Tonatiuh qualo.

2.

In iquac muchiua hi, chichiliuhtimomana, aoc

3.   4.   5.

tlacamani. aoc tlacaca. ça mocuecueptimani. cenca

6.   7.   8.

tlacoçavia: niman yc tlatzomoni. tlacatl comoni,

9.   10.   11.   12.

neacomanalo, necomonilo. nemauhtilo, nechoquililo,

13.   14.

tlachoquiztleua ỹ macevalti, netenviteco. netempapa-

15.   16.   17.

uilo, tlacauaca. tlacauatzalo. tzâtziua, oyoualli mo-

18.   19.   20.   21.

teca. Tlacaztalmicoa, malmicoa, neçoa. tlacoq'xtilo,

22.   23.   24.   25.

nenacazteco: Auh yn teteupan xuxuchcuico, tlacha-

26.   27.   28.   29.

lantoc, tlacauacatoc. Yc mitoaya, yntla tlamiz, yn

30.   31.   32.   33.

qualo tonatiuh, centlayouaz: valtemuzque yn tzitzi-

34.

tzimi. tequaquiui.—

1.   2.

Eclipsase el sol ponerse colorado. p̃t.° ochichiliuhti-

3.

momã. turbarse el sol o el agua. p̃t.° aoc otlacaman.

4.

turbarse la persona. p̃t.° aoc otlacacatca. rebuluerse o

estarse remeçiendo. p̃t. omocuecueptimãca. omocue-

6.

cueptiman. amarillecerse el sol. o los mayzales qñ

7.

estan pa colarse p̃t.° otlacoçauix. alborotarse la

8.

gente. p̃t.° otlatzomon. lo mis.° p̃t.° otlacatl comon.

9.   10.

lo mismo. p̃t. oneacomanaloc. lo mismo. pret.° oneco-

11.   12.

moniloc. todos temen. p̃t.° onemauiztiloc. todos

lloran a vozes. p̃t.° onechoquililoc. otlachoquiztleuac.

13.   14.

todos dan grita. p̃t.° onetenvitecoc. lo mismo. p̃t.°

15.

onetempapauiloc. todos dã alaridos. p̃t.° otlacauacac.

16.

lo mismo. p̃t. otlacauatzaloc. todos dã vozes. p̃t.°

17.

otzatziuac. todos vozean por todas ptes. p̃t. oyoualli-

their ears with maguey spines and passed flexible twigs or the like through the holes which the spines had made. And then, in all the temples, they sang and sounded [musical instruments], making a great din. And they said: "If the sun becometh completely eclipsed, nevermore will he give light; eternal darkness will fall, and the demons will come down. They will come to eat us!"

hecho. Y luego por todos los templos cantauan y tañian haziendo gran ruido. Y dezian si del todo se acaba de eclipsar el sol nunca mas alumbrara ponerse han perpetuas tinieblas y descenderan los demonios vendran nos a comer.

Second Chapter.

When the moon newly appeareth, he seemeth like a thin, little curve of wire. He doth not yet shine. By little and little he goeth growing. On the fifteenth day he is full. And when now he is full, he cometh forth in the east at sunset. He seemeth like a great millstone—very round and very red. And as he goeth rising, he becometh white or shining. [There is what] looketh like a rabbit in the middle of him. And if there are no clouds he shineth almost like the

Capitulo Segũdo

Quando la luna nuevamẽte nace, parece como vn arquito de alambre delgado aun no resplandece: poco a poco va creciendo. A los quinze dias es llena. Y qñ ya es llena sale por el oriente a la puesta del sol: parece como vna rueda de molino grande muy redonda y muy colorada. Y qñ va subiendo se para blanca o resplandeziente: parece como vn conejo en medio della. Y si no ay nubes resplandece casi como el sol, casi como de dia. Y d'spues de llena cũpli-

ILLUSTRATIONS

¶ la fabula del coneio que esta en la lu
na: es esta. Dizen, que los dioses seburla-
ron con la luna y dieron la con un coneio en la cara, y que dsso le el coneio señalado en la cara: y con esto le escurecieron la cara como con un ardenal
despues desso salio ya alumbrar al
mundo. Dezian, que antes que ouiese
dia enel mundo que iuntaron los dioses
en aquel lugar que se llama teutioaca,
(que es el pueblo de san Juan entre chicunauhtlan y otumba) dixeron los u-
nos a los otros. Dioses, quien tendra cargo de alumbrar almundo? luego a estas palabras respondio un dios que se
llamaua tecucijtecatl y dixo. Yo tomo a cargo de alumbrar almundo.
luego otraues hablaron los dioses y dixeron quien sera otro? luego se miraro
los unos a los otros, y conferian quien
seria el otro. Y minguno dellos osaua
ofrecerse aaquel ofi todos temian y
se escusaban. Uno dellos dioses de q
no se hazia cuenta y era buboso, no hablaua sino oya lo que los otros dioses
dezian. Y los otros hablaron le y dixe-
le: Se tu el que alumbres bubosito. y el
de buena Voluntad obedecio alo que le
mandaron y respondio, en mrd recibo
lo que me aueis mandado se assi. y luego los dos comencaron a hazer penitencia quatro dias.

¶ Bzcatqui ytlatlatollo, ymic nnitoa
yuhqmin tochton yxco Vetztoc metztli. Inhin, quilmach caic ycn onne-
abiltiloc, ycomxminitecque, ycn
mixtlatlatzoque; ycomxpopoloque
ycomixomictique yntetzo çiquac
catepan oquiçaco, omomanaco.
Mitoa ynocyouaya, inayamo tona, inayamo tlathui, quilmach mocentlalique, monooztque ynteteo
ynimpa teutinaca, qintoque, q
molhuique. Haxiualhuia teteoe
aquin tlatquiz, aquin tlamama
yntonaz, yntlathuiz? Auhinma
yeic yehuatl uncan ontlatoa, o
mxquetza ynteaicijtecatl, qto.
teteoe canehuatl niyez. Ocappa
quitoque ynteteu, aquin occe?
Nima yeicne panotl mohotta, q
mottitia, quimolhuia quen oyezhi,
quentoyezque? Ayac mottlapalo
aya, ynocce omixquetzaz: camu
chitlacatl momauhtiaya, mqcaya.
Auh amo onnextiticata yca tlacatl
iianaVatzn uncan teuan tlacacti
catca innenonotzalo: nima ycyeh
uatl connotzque teteo, quilhuiq.
tehuatl tiyez nanaVatze. Nima q
cuitiuetz yntlatolli, quipaccaceli
qnito, cayequalli teteoe oanech
mocnelilique. Nima ycompeual-
tique inyca tlamaceua, mocauhq
naVilhuitl omextin teteaicijte-
1 ratl

¶ Estar aqui. o he aqui. pto
yzocatca. 2. Nueuas. o ablillas. caso no tlatlatollo. 3. bur
o dizer. 4. iugar. o burlar. pt
ominauilti. 5. herir en la cara
pt. omiteixhuinc. ixhuiute.
omiteixtlatlazon. o. borrar.
o amanzillar. o raer la sobre
haz de alguna cosa. pt. omie
popolo. o. amortiguar la cara
pt. omiteixomicti. onixomic.
8. dezirse. pt. omito. 9. antes
que comenca se el dia. 10. antes
que resplandeciese el sol. pt.
otonac. 11. antes que anine-
ciese. pt. otlathuic. 12. Iunta
se o congregarse. pt. oninocl
tlali. 13. hablar se o entrarse e
conse. pt. oninononoh. deliberar comigo mismo. 14. lugar o
llamado. 15. dezir unos a otros a
go. pt. omicnolhui. dezir asimi
15. Venir aca. pt. oniualla. 17.
en. 18. lleuar a cuestas o tener
cargo de algo. pt. onitlatquic.
onitlamama. 19. enel mismo lugu
o tpo. 20. presentar se alguno
delante de otro. pt. onimixquetl
21. nobre yprio de un dios y de
la luna. 22. Yo. 23. Ser algo
onicatca. 24. quien otro. 25. u-
nos a otros. 26. mirarse unea
otros. pt. oninohottac. mirarse
por todas ptes. 27. conferir im
si. pt. onicnotthi. conferir com
go mismo 22. como sera esto. 29
como nos determinaremos. 30.n
guno. 31. osar. o atreuerse. ptd
ominotlapalo. 32. todos. 33. temu
pt. ominomauhti. 34. escusarse
pt. oninetinquiz. 35. parecerse o
estar eminente. pt. oninexticat
36. Nombre de un dios que era
buboso. y nombre de la mesina e
fermedad. 37. conlos otros. 38.
estar oyendo. pt. onitlacacchca
39. arrebatar. pt. oniccuitiuecl
40. recebir de buena voluntad
pt. onitlapaccaceli. 41. Esta bie.p
42. hazer mrd. o bnificio. p. oni
tlacneli. 43. luego. 44. comen-
car. pt. onitlapeualti. 45. h yo
pnia. pt. onitlamaceuh. 46
ambos.

Page from *Memoriales con Escolios* (Chapter 2)

porque el que mas podia correr,
que otros, tomaua la tea de pino:
y ansi muy presto, casi en vn mo
mento llegauan, a sus pueblos: y
luego venian, a tomar to
dos los vezinos della. y era cosa
de ver, la mucha dumbre de
los fuegos, entodos los pueblos,
que parecia ser de dia: y pri
mero se hazian lumbres, en
las casas, donde morauan,
los dichos ministros, delos ydo
los.

C Capitulo doze. de co
mo la gente, despues de
auer tomado, fuego nu
euo, renouauan todos
sus vestidos, y alhajas:
donde se pone la figura
de la cuenta de los años.

De la dicha manera, hecha
la lumbre nueua, luego los ve
zinos, de cada pueblo, en cada
casa, renouauan sus alhajas:
y los hombres y mugeres, se ves
tian de vestidos nueuos, y po
nian enel suelo, nueuos peta
tes

ca quitototzaia, quimotlaloch
tiaia: inic teiuhca caxitzque in
chan, quimomamacatiquiça, qui
mocuicuilitiquiça, ic mopapa tla
tiui. Amo uecauh, amo machiztli.
canisquichcauitl, y, in coñaxitia
ia, in quicueponaltiaia: çanachi
tonca innouiiampa, cuecuepoca
timoteca tletl, cuecuepocatiqui
ca: no vmpa achto quitquitiqui
ca, quitlamelaoaltitiuetzi inin
teupan, inincalmecac, inincacal
pulco: çatepan ic moiaoa, tepan
cēmani in nouiian tlatlaxilacal
pan, yoan in calpan.

C Inic matlactlomume.
capitulo, vncan mitoa: in que
nin inisquich tlacatl, inicoac
omocuic in iancuic tletl: auh
inicoac, y, muchi tlacatl, quiia
cuiliaia initlaquen, yoan in
isquich cali tlatquitl.

C Niman icoac, isquich ian
cuiia, in cali tlatquitl: in oquich
tlatquitl, in cioatlatquitl, in
petlatl, in tolcuestli, inicpalli:
muchi iancuic in moteteca, ioā
in tenamaztli, in texolotl. No
iquac iancuic nequentilo, nel

—*After Paso y Troncoso*

1. Sun
2. Moon
3. The rabbit in the moon
4. Eclipse of the moon
5. Comet
6. Comet's tail

7. Stars
8. The Winds
9-10. Lightning
11. Clouds
12. Rainbow

—After Paso y Troncoso

13. Ice, snow, and hail
14. Storing food against famine
15. Delivering children into bondage
16. Boring new fire on the breast of a sacrificial victim

17. New fire in the temples
18. New fire taken to homes
19. Breaking and throwing away household goods at the end of the fifty-two-year cycle

The Calendar Wheel

This table placed above [opposite] is the year count, and it is a most ancient thing. They say that its inventor was Quetzalcoatl. It proceedeth in this way: they begin with the east, which is where the reeds are (or, according to others, with the south, where the rabbit is) and say One Reed. And thence they go to the north, where the flint is, and they say Two Flint Knife. Then they go to the west, where the house is, and there they say Three House. And then they go to the north, which is where the rabbit is, and they say Four Rabbit. And then they turn to the east, and say Five Reed. And thus they go, making four revolutions, until they reach thirteen, so that they end where they began. And then they return to one, saying One Flint Knife. And in this way, making revolutions, they assign thirteen years to each of the characters, or to each of the four quarters of the world. And then fifty-two years are completed, which is a bundle of years, when the Jubilee is celebrated and new fire is made in the manner set forth above [Chapters 9-12]. Then they again count as at the beginning. It should be noted that they disagree a great deal, in various places, as to the beginning of the year. In some parts, they told me that it began at some date in January; in others, that [it was] at the beginning of February; in others, that [it was] some time in March. In Tlatilulco I gathered together many old men, the most able ones whom I could secure, and, along with the most able of the college students, this matter was discussed for many days. And they all concluded that the year began on the second day of February.

Esta table, arriba puesta: es la cuenta de los años, y es cosa antiquissima. Dizen, que el inuentor della, fue Quetzalcoatl: procede desta manera: que comiençan del Oriente, que es donde estã las cañas: y segun otros, del medio dia, donde esta el conejo, y dizen ce acatl: y de alli van al Norte, donde esta el pedernal, y dizen vme tecpatl: luego van al occidente, donde esta la Casa, y alli dizen iey calli: y luego van al abrego, que es donde esta el conejo, y dizen naui tochtli: y luego tornan al oriente, y dizen macuilli acatl. Y ansi van dando quatro bueltas, hasta que llegan a treze, que se acaban a donde començo: y luego bueluen a vno, diziendo ce tecpatl. I desta manera, dando bueltas: dan treze años, a cada vno de los caracteres, o a cada vna, de las quatro partes, del mundo. I entõce, se cumplen. 52. años, que es vna gauilla de años: donde se celebra, el Iubileo, y se saca lumbre nueua, en la forma arriba puesta: luego bueluen a contar como de principio. Es de notar, que discrepan mucho, en diuersos lugares del principio del año: en vnas partes me dixeron, que començaua a tantos de Enero: en otras, que a primero de hebrero: en otras, que a tantos de Março: En el tlatilulco, junte muchos viejos: los mas diestros, que yo pude auer, y juntamente, con los mas habiles de los colegiales, se alterco esta materia por muchos dias: y todos ellos concluyeron, que començaua el año, segũdo dia de Hebrero.

Inicome parrapho ypāmitoa injntoca yntlacpac eecatiepac nittchivo

Inic yai parrapho ypan mitoa ynxiuhpovalli:

(16)

(13)

(17)

(14)

(18)

Inipani omacatl dnpa ipan m vmpoalxiuh vmome.

xiuhtonali mo pilia intoxiuh tica omatlactli

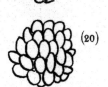

(19)

(15)

(20)

—*After Paso y Troncoso*

22. Natural Phenomena and year signs, from *Primeros Memoriales,* Cap. 2

13. Wind	17. Frost	*Year signs, beginning at top*
14. Lightning bolt	18. Cloud	One Rabbit
15. Rain	19. Snow	Two Reed
16. Rainbow	20. Hail	Three Flint Knife
		Four House

18.
motecac. Sacrificar hombres blancos. p̃t.º otlacaztal-
19.   20.
micoac. Sacrificar captiuos. p̃. omalmicoac. Vntarse
                                      21.
cõ la sangre de las oreias los rostros. p̃t. oneçoac. pasar
                                22.
mimbres por las oreias. p̃. otlacoq'xtiloc. hazer cor-

taduras ẽ las oreias pa sacar sangre. pret.º onenacaz-
          23.   24.
tecoc. Por todos los templos. cantar cantares q̃ se
                    25.
llamã xuchcuicatl. hazer ruydo. p̃. otlachalantoca.
    26.   27. 28. 29.
dar alaridos. p̃. otlacavacatoca. Por tanto. si. acavase
              30.   31.
algo. p̃. otlan. Vt. sup̃. ponerse ppetua oscuridad. p̃.
          32.   33.
ocẽtlayouac. descender. p̃. onivaltemuc. demonio. o
                    34.
diablo. ca. notzitzimiuh. comer hombres. p̃t. onite-

qua.

1.

Metztli. tecuciztecatl.

2.
Yn iquac yancuican valmomana coltontli yuhquin
3.   4.
teçacanecuilli, teçacanecuiltontli, ayamo tlanextia:
5.   6.   7.
çan yuiyan veixtiuh, malacachiuhtiuh. teuilacachiuh-
          8.   9.
tiuh. Caxtoltica ỹ vel malacachiui, teuilacachiui, yn
    10.   11.
vel maci, yn chicaua. Auh yn iquac vel oyaualiuh,

omalacachiuh, ynic valneci, ynic valmomana yn
12.   13.   14.
vmpa yquiçayan tonatiuh yn iquac ye tlapoyaua
15.   16.   17.   18.
yuhquin comalli, veipol, vel teuilacachtic, malacach-

1.

Luna.

2.   3.
Arquillo. barbute a manera de medio arq'llo. caso.
                                    4.   5.
notẽçacanecuil. notẽçacanecuilton. aun no. poco a
          6.   7.
poco. yrse. engrandeciendo. p̃t.º oueixtia. yrse.

haziendo redondo. p̃t.º omalacachiuhtia. oteuilaca-
          8.   9.
chiuhtia. a los quinze dias. acabarse de aredondear.

pret.º oyaualiuh. omalacachiuh. oteuilacachiuh. per-
    10.   11.
fecionarse. p̃t.º omacic. hazerse fuerte. p̃t.º ochicauac.
12.   13.   14.
aculla. a la salida. caso. noquiçaya. a la tarde. o a la

sun; [it is] almost as daytime. And after he hath become completely full, by little and little he goeth waning until he becometh as he was when he began. They then say: "Now the moon dieth; now he sleepeth." This is when he riseth with the dawn at the time of the conjunction. They say: "Now the moon is dead."

damente poco a poco se va menguando hasta que se va a hazer como quando começo: dizen entonces ya se muere la luna, ya se duerme Esto es quando sale ya con el alua al tp̃o de la coniuncion: dizen ya es muerta la luna.

19.
tic, yuhquin tlapalli chichiltic, chichilpatic. Auh q'ni-
20.   21.   22.   23.
quac in ye achi quiualtoca, in ye ualacoq'ça iztaya:
24.
mitoa ye tlachia, ye tlanextia ȳ metztli, ye metztona:
25.   26.   27.
yztalectic vel iztac, ynic motta ynic neci iuhq̃n
28. 29. 30. 31.
tochton yxco vetztoc. Yntlacamo tle mixtli. ȳtlacamo
32.
mixxoa. mixtemi. yuhquī tona yc tlaneci, mitoa
33.   34.   35.
yehon cemilhuitl vel tlanaltona. tlanaltonatimani.
36.
tlacalantoc. tlacalantimani. Auh yn iquac ouelacic.
37.   38.   39.
ouelmacic. ytlanextiliz ȳ izquilhuitl yc veya, malaca-
40.   41.   42.
chiui: çan iuh nenti oc ceppa tepitonaui, tepitonauh-

tiuh, oc ceppa yuhqui mochiua ynic yãcuican
43. 44.
valmomana, çan iuiyã poliui, poliuhtiuh: mitoa ye
45.   46.
õmiqui ȳ metztli ye ve in quicochi, ye ve in ic cochi
47.   48.
ye tlathuitiuh, ye tlathuinavac ȳ valquiça. Auh yn

iquac vel ompoliuh, mitoa õmic ȳ metztli:—

15.   16.
puesta. del sol. asi como. comal. caso nocomal. Es vna
torta de barro cozido en que cuezen las tortillas.
17.   18.
grandazo. cosa redonda. y llana. caso. noteuilacach.
19.   20.   21.
cosa muy colorada. vn poco. proceder. p̃t. oquiualto-
22.   23.
cac. se sube en alto. p̃t.º oualacoquiz. pararse blanca.
24.
p̃t. oyztaz. resplandecer. p̃t.º otlachix. otlanexti.
25.   26.
ometztonac. cosa blanquezina. cosa muy blanca.
27.   28.   29.
parecer. omottac. onez. coneioelo. en la cara. caso.
30.   31.
nixco. estar echado. pret.º ouetztoca. Si ninguna cosa.
32.   33. 34. 35.
anublarse. p̃t. omixxoac. omixtẽ. casi. dia. resplandecer mucho, o echar mucha claridad de si. p̃t.º otla-
naltonac. otlanaltonatimanca, otlacalantoca, otlaca-
36.
lantia. cumplirse o perfecionarse p̃t.º oacic. omacic.
37.
resplandor. o claridad. caso. notlanex. notlanextiliz.
38.   39.   40.
tantos. engrandecerse. o crecer. p̃t.º oueix. poco. a
41.   42.
poco. otra vez. achicarse o menguarse p̃t.º otepito-
43.   44.
nauh. otepitonauhtia. poco a poco. desaparecer.
45.   46.
opoliuh. opoliuhtia. morirse. p̃t.º onimic. dormir
47.   48.
mucho. p̃t.º onicoch. amanecer. p̃t.º otlathuic. iunto al

alua.

This is the tale of the rabbit which is in the moon. They say that the gods played tricks on the moon and struck him in the face with a rabbit; and the rabbit remained marked upon his face. And with it they darkened his face as if with a weal. Thereafter he came forth to light the world. They said that, before there was day in the world, the gods came together in that place which is named Teotihuacan (which is the town of San Juan, between Chico-nauhtlan and Otumba). They said to one another: "O gods, who will have the burden of lighting the world?" Then to these words answered a god named Tecuciztecatl, and he said: "I shall take the burden of lighting the world." Then once more the gods spoke, and they said: "Who will be another?" Then they looked at one another, and deliberated on who the other would be. And none of them dared offer himself for that office; all were afraid and declined. One of the gods, to whom no one was paying attention, and who was covered with pustules, did not speak but listened to what the other gods were saying. And the others spoke to him and said to him:

La fabula del coneio que esta en la luna: es esta. Dizen, que los dioses se burlaron con la luna y die-ronla con vn coneio en la cara, y quedole el coneio señalado en la cara: y con esto le escurecieron la cara como con vn cardenal. Despues desso salio pa alum-brar al mundo. Dezian, que antes que ouiese dia en el mundo que iuntaron los dioses en aquel lugar que se llama teutioacã, (que es el pueblo de San Juan entre chicunauhtlan y otumba) dixeron los vnos a los otros. Dioses, quien tendra cargo de alumbrar al mundo? luego a estas palabras respondio vn dios que se llamaua Tecuciztecatl y dixo. Yo tomo a cargo de alumbrar al mundo. Luego otra vez hablaron los dioses y dixeron quien sera otro? Luego se mirarõ los vnos a los otros, y conferian quien seria el otro. Y ninguno dellos osaua ofrecerse a aquel ofi.º todos temian y se escusavan. Vno dellos dioses de q̃ no se hazia cuẽta y era buboso, no hablaua sino oya lo que los otros dioses dezian. Y los otros hablaronle y dixerõle: Se tu el que alumbres bubosito. Y el de buena voluntad obedecio a lo que le mandaron y respondio, en mrd reçibo lo que me aveis mandado

1.   2.
Izcatqui ytlatlatollo, ynic mitoa yuhquin tochton
3.
yxco vetztoc metztli. Jn hin, quilmach ça ic yca
4.   5.
onneaviltiloc, yc conixuiuitecque, yc conixtlatlatzo-
6.   7.
que; yc conixpopoloque yc conixomictique yn teteo
8.
ỹ iquac çatepan oquiçaco, omomanaco. Mitoa yn oc
9.   10.   11.
youayã, in ayamo tona, in ayamo tlathui, quilmach
12.   13.   14.
mocentlalique, mononotzque ỹ teteo yn vmpa teuti-
15.   16.
uacã, quitoque, q'molhiuque. Tla xiualhuiã teteoé
17.   18.
aquin tlatquiz, aquin tlamamaz. yn tonaz, yn tla-
19.   20.
thuiz? Auh nimã ye ic yehuatl vncan ontlatoa, õmix-
21.   22.   23.
quetza yn tecuciztecatl, q'to. teteoé ca nehuatl niyez.
24.
Oc ceppa quitoque yn teteu, aquin oc ce? Nimã ye
25.   26.   27.
ic nepanotl mohotta, q'mottitia, quimolhuia quen
28.   29.   30.   31.
õyez hi, quen tõyezque? Ayac motlapaloaya, yn oc
32.   33.
ce õmixquetzaz: çã muchi tlacatl momauhtiaya,
34.   35.   36.
tzinq'çaya. Auh amo onnezticatca ỹ ce tlacatl nanava-
37.   38.
tzin vncan teuan tlacacticatca innenonotzalo: nimã

yc yehvatl connotzque ỹ teteo, quilhuiq̃. tehuatl tiyez
39.   40.
nanavatze. Nimã q'cuitiuetz yn tlatolli, quipaccaceli
41.   42.   43.
quito, ca ye qualli teteoe oãnechmocnelilique. Nimã
44.   45.
yc compeualtique in ye tlamaceua, moçauhq navil-
46.
huitl omextin ỹ tecuciztecatl Auh nimã no yquac

1.
Estar aqui. o he aqui. p̃t.° yz ocatca. 2. Nueuas. o
ablillas. caso notlatlatollo. 3. diz̃q. o dizen. 4. iugar.
o burlar. p̃t.° oninauilti. 5. herir en la cara. p̃t.° oniteixhuitec. ixhuiuitec. oniteixtlatlatzon. 6. borrar. o
amanzillar. o raer la sobrehaz de alguna cosa. p̃t.°
oniq'xpopolo. 7. amortiguar la cara. p̃t.° oniteixô-
micti. onixômic. 8. dezirse. p̃t.° omito. 9. antes que
començase el dia. 10. ãtes que resplandeciese el sol.
p̃t.° otonac. 11. antes que amaneciese. p̃t.° otlathuic.
12. Juntarse o congregarse. p̃t.° oninocẽtlali. 13. ha-
blarse o entrarse ẽ consejo. p̃t.° oninononotz. deliberar
cõmigo mismo. 14. lugar asi llamado. 15. dezir vnos
a otros algo. p̃t.° onicnolhui. dezir a si mis.° 16. venir
aca. p̃t.° oniualla. 17. q'en. 18. lleuar a cuestas o tener
cargo de algo. p̃t.° onitlatquic. onitlamama. 19. en
el mismo lugar o tp̃o. 20. presentarse alguno delante
de otro. p̃t.° oninixquetz. 21. nõbre pprio de vn dios
y de la luna. 22. yo. 23. Ser algo. p̃t. onicatca.
24. quien otro? 25. Vnos a otros. 26. mirarse vnos a
otros. p̃t.° oninohottac. mirarse por todas ptes. 27. conferir ẽtre si. p̃t.° onicnottiti. conferir comigo mismo.
28. como sera esto? 29. como nos determinaremos.

"You be the one who is to give light, little pustule-covered one." And right willingly he obeyed what they commanded, and he answered: "Thankfully I accept what you have commanded me [to do]. Let it be [as you say]." And then both began to perform penances for four days.

And then they lit a fire in the hearth which was made on a crag (which now they call *teotexcalli*). [As for] the god named Tecuciztecatl, all which he offered was costly. Instead of branches he offered precious feathers named *quetzalli*. And instead of balls of straw he offered balls of gold. And instead of maguey spines he offered spines made of precious stones. And instead of bloodied spines, he offered spines made of red coral. And the copal incense which he offered was very good. And the pustule-covered one, who was named Nanauatzin, in place of branches offered green rushes tied in threes—in all amounting to nine. And he offered balls of straw and maguey spines, and he bloodied them with his own blood. And instead of copal incense he offered the scabs from his pustules. For each of these was raised a tower like a mountain. On these same mountains they did penance four nights. (Today these moun-

se assi. Y luego los dos començaron a hazer penitencia quatro dias.

Y luego encendieron fuego ẽ el hogar el qual era hecho ẽ vna peña (que agora llaman teutexcalli). El dios llamado Tecuciztecatl todo lo que ofrecia era precioso: en lugar de ramos ofrecia plumas ricas que se llamã quetzalli. Y en lugar de pelotas de heno, ofrecia pelotas de oro: y en lugar de espinas de maguei ofrecia espinas hechas de piedras preciosas: y en lugar de espinas ẽsangrentadas, ofrecia espinas hechas de coral colorado: y el copal que ofrecia era muy bueno. Y el buboso que se llamaua Nanauatzin en lugar de ramos ofrecia cañas verd's atadas de tres en tres, todas ellas llegauan a nueue: y ofrecia bulas de heno y espinas de maguei, y ensangrentaualas con su misma sangre: y ẽ lugar de copal ofrecia las postillas de las bobas. A cada vno destos se les edifico vna torre como mõte, en los mismos montes hizierõ penitencia quatro noches agora se llamã estos mõtes tzacualli. estan ambos cabe el pu.º de s. Ju.º que se llama teu-

44

47. 48. 49. 50.

motlali yn tletl ye tlatla yn vncan tlecuilco quitoca-

yotia yn tlecuilli teutexcalli. Auh in yehuatl tecuciz-
                                        51.   52.
tecatl yn ipan tlamaceuaya muchi tlaçotli: yn iacxo-
          53.   54.   55.
yauh quetzalli, auh yn içacatapayol teocuitlatl, yn
56.   57.   58.   59.
iuitz chalchiuitl, ȳyc tlaezhuilli, tlaezçotilli tapachtli,
          60.   61.
auh yn icopal vel yeh yn copalli. Auh ȳ nanavatzin
                    62.   63.
ȳ iacxoyauh mochiuh çan acatl xoxouhqui, acaxo-
          64.   65.   66.
xouhqui, eeyn tlalpilli, tlacuitlalpilli. nepan chicu-
              67.
navi in ye muchi, auh yn içacatapayol çan yeeh yn
                                68.
ocoçacatl, auh yn iuitz çan ye no yeh ȳ mevitztli, auh

ȳic quezhuiaya uel yeh yn iezço, auh yn icopal çan
          69.   70.
yeh yn inanavauh concocoleuaya. Yn omextin hin,
71.   72.
cecentetl ȳtepeuh muchiuh, yn vmpa ontlamaceuhti-
                                        73.
nenca nauhyoval (mitoa ȳ axcan tetepe tzacualli,

ytzacual tonatiuh yoã yztacual metztli). Auh yn
                                        74.
õtzonquiz nauhyoval yntlamaceualiz, niman quitla-

tlaçato, quimamayavito yn imacxoyauh yoan in ye

muchi ypan otlamaceuhque. Jn hin mochiuh ye

30. n[in]guno.[21] 31. osar, o atreuerse. pret. oninotlapalo. 32. todos. 33. temer. p̃t.º oninomauhti. 34. escusarse. p̃t.º onitzinquiz. 35. parecerse. o estar eminente.
p̃t.º oninezticat[ca]. 36. Nombre de vn dios que era
buboso. y nombre de la mesma ẽfermedad. 37. con los
otros. 38. estar oyendo. p̃t.º onitlacacticati. 39. arrebatar. p̃t.º oniccuitiuetz. 40. recibir de buena voluntad.
p̃t.º onitlapaccaceli. 41. Esta bien. 42. hazer mrd. o
bñficio. p̃. onitlacneli. 43. luego. 44. començar. p̃t.º
onitlapeualti. 45. hazer pñia. p̃t.º onitlamaceuh. 46.
ambos. 47. fuego. caso Notleuh. 48. arder. p̃t.º onitla-
tlac. 49. hogar. caso notlecuil. 50. nombrar. p̃t.º onite-
tocayoti. 51. cosa preciosa, o rara. 52. ramo de vn
arbol. caso Nacxoyauh. 53. pluma rica. caso noque-
tzal. 54. pelota de heno. ca.º noçacatapayol. 55. oro.
cas. noteocuitl. 56. espina de qualquiera. cas. nouitz.
57. vn gño. de piedra preciosa, que es verde. ca.
nochalchiuh. 58. cosa ensangretada. 59. coral, o ava-
nera colorada. caso. Notapach. 60. encienso desta
tierra. ca. nocopal. 61. persona bubosa. 62. caña. ca.º
nacauh. 63. cosa verde, o cruda. 64. de tres en tres.
65. cosa atada. caso Notlalpil. notlacuitlalpil. 66. cosa
iunta. 67. todo. 68. espina de maguei. ca. novitz.
nomevitz. 69. buba. caso. nonanavauh. 70. leuantar

21. In photographing, some letters were lost at the end of lines. We have supplied a number of those missing.

tains are called *tzacualli;* they are both near the town of San Juan, which is called Teotihuacan.) After they ended their four nights of penance, then they threw away the branches and all else with which they had performed penances.

This was done at the end, or at the conclusion, of the penitence, when, the next night—at midnight—they were to begin to perform their offices. And a little before midnight [the other gods] gave them their adornment. To the one named Tecuciztecatl they gave a feather [headdress] called *aztacomitl* and a linen jacket. And [as for] the pustule-covered one named Nanauatzin, they covered his head with [a] paper [headdress] called *amatzontli,* and put upon him a stole of paper and a paper breech clout. And midnight having come, all the gods placed themselves about the hearth, called *teotexcalli.* In this place the fire blazed four days. The aforementioned gods arranged themselves in two rows, some at one side of the fire, some at the other side. And then the two [gods] above mentioned placed themselves before the fire, facing the fire, between the two rows of gods, all of whom were standing. And then the gods

tiuacã. Desque se acabaron las quatro noches de su pnĩa, luego echarõ por ay los ramos

y todo lo de mas con que hizieron la pnĩa. Esto se hizo al fin, o al remate de su pnĩa, quando la noche siguiẽte a la media noche avian de comẽçar a hazer sus oficios. Y ante vn poco de la media noche dieronles sus adereços. A aquel que se llamava tecuciztecatl dierõ vn plumaje llamado aztacomitl y vna xaqueta de lienço: y al buboso que se llama nanavatzin tocaronle la cabeça cõ papel q̃ se llama amatzontli, y pusierõle vna stola de papel y vn maxtli de papel. Y llegada la media noche todos los dioses se pusieron en deredor del hogar que se llama teutexcalli en este lugar ardio el fuego quatro dias: ordenaronse los dhos dioses en dos rencles, vnos de la vna pte del fuego, otros de la otra pte. Y luego los dos sobredhos se pusieron delante del fuego, las caras hazia el fuego en medio de las dos rencles de los dioses: los quales todos estauã leuãtados. Y luego hablaron los dioses y dixeron a tecuciztecatl. Ea pues

75.

inneevalco, yquac in ye valyoua tlacotizque, teotiz-

que. Auh yn iquac ye onaci youalnepantla, niman ye
      76.   77.

ic quintlamamaca, quinchichiua, quincencava: yn
          78.   79.

tecuciztecatl quimacaque yaztacon mimiltic yoan
80.   81.

yxicol: auh yn nanaoatzin çan amatl ynic cõquailpi-
                82.   83.

que, contzonilpique ytoca yamatzon, yoan yamanea-
        84.   85.

panal, yoan yamamaxtli. Auh in ye iuhqui, yn ouel-
                          86.

açic yovalnepantla, ỹ muchintin teteu quiyaualotimo-

manque yn tlecuilli, ỹ moteneua teutexcalli, yn vncan
                87.   88.

navilhuitl otlatlac tletl, nenecoc motecpãque: auh
  89.   90.

nepãtla quimõmanq, quimonquetzque ỹ omextin hĩ,
                                91.

moteneua ỹ tecuciztecatl yoã nanaoatzin, quixnamic-

timomanque, quixnamictimoq̃tzque yn tlecuilli. Auh

niman ye ic tlatoah yn teteu, quilhuique yn tecuciz-
      92.   93.

tecatl. O tlacuele tecuciztecatle, xonhuetzi, xõmoma-

yaui ỹ tleco: nimã ye ic yauh momayauiz yn tleco.

---

algo que esta pegado a otra cosa. o desapegar. p̃t.º
oniccoleuh. 71. cada vno suyo. 72. torre, o cerro. ca.
notepeuh. 73. nombre proprio de aquellas torres. caso.
notzacual. 74. arrojar, o desechar. p̃t.º onictlaz.
onicmayauh.

75. remate o fin de tiempo en el qual se hazia pnĩa.
76. dar le vestir, o de comer a otro. p̃t.º onictlamama-
cac, onictlamacac. 77. atauiar o adereçar. p̃t.º onitechi-
chiuh. onitecencauh. 78. plumaje como cãtaro hecho
de pluma blanca de la ave q̃ se dize aztatl. caso. naz-
tacon. 79. cosa roliza. 80. xaqueta sin mancas. caso.
noxicol. 81. atar. o tocar la cabeça. onitequailpi. oni-
tetzonilpi. 82. cabellos de papel. ca. namatzon. 83.
stola de papel. caso. namaneapã. namaneapanal.
noneamaneapanal. 84. maxtli de papel. ca. nama-
maxtli. 85. llegar. p̃t.º oacic. 86. cercar ē derredor.
p̃t.º onicyavalotimoman. o ponerse psonas ē cerco de
alguna cosa. 87. de ãbas ptes. 88. ponerse en orden
psonas. p̃t.º oninotecpã. 89. en medio. 90. ponerse
algũas psonas en pie en lugar aparente. p̃t.º oniqui-
mõman. oniquimõquetz. 91. ponerse algunas psonas
en pie fronteros de alguna cosa. p̃t.º oniquixnamic-
timoq̃tz. no se dize oniquixnamictimomã. 92. ea pues

spoke, and said to Tecuciztecatl: "How now, Tecuciztecatl! Go into the fire!" And then he braced himself to cast himself into the fire.

And since the fire was large and blazed high, as he felt the great heat of the fire, he became frightened and dared not cast himself into the fire. He turned back. Once more he turned to throw himself into the fire, making an effort and drawing nearer, to cast himself into the flames. But, feeling the great heat, he held back and dared not cast himself [into it]. Four times he tried, but never let himself go. A rule [had been] made not to try more than four times. Since he had tried four times, the gods then spoke to Nanauatzin, and said to him: "How now, Nanauatzin! You try!" And when the gods had addressed him, he exerted himself, and with closed eyes undertook [the ordeal] and cast himself into the flames. And then he began to crackle and pop in the fire like one who is roasted.

tecuciztecatl entra tu en el fuego. Y el luego acometio pa echarse en el fuego.

Y como el fuego era grande y estaua muy encendido, como sintio el gran calor del fuego, ouo miedo no oso echarse en el fuego, boluiose atras: otra vez torno para echarse en el fuego haziendose fuerça, y llegandose mas acerca para echarse en el fuego: pero sintiendo el calor grande detuuose, no oso echarse. Quatro vezes prouo, pero nunca se dejo echar: estaua puesto mãdamj.° que no prouarse mas de quatro vezes. Desque ouo prouado quatro vezes los dioses luego hablaron a nanauatzin y dixeronle. Ea pues nanauatzin prueua tu. Y como le ouieron hablado los dioses, esforçose y cerrado los ojos arremetio y echose en el fuego. Y luego començo a rechinar y respendar en el fuego como quien se asa. Y como vio tecuciztecatl

o alto pues. 93. arrojarse. p̃t.º onõvetz. onõnoma-

yauh.—

94.   95.

Auh yn itech oaçito totonillotl yn amo yxnamiquiztli,

yn amo yecoliztli, amo yhiyouiliztli ynic cenca vel
   96.   97

oxoxotlac tlecuilli, ovel vahualantimotlali, ovel mo-
            98.   99.

tlatlali yn tletl: yc çã ommixmauhtito, õmotilque-
        100.

tzato, valtzinquiz, valtziniloth: ye no ceppa yauh

94. calor. caso Nototonillo. nototoca. 95. cosa no

sufrible. cosa intolerable. 96. encenderse mucho el

fuego. p̃t.º oxoxotlac. 97. estar hecho gran fuego. vn

gran monton de brasas. p̃t.º ovahualantimotlali. omo-

tlâtlali. 98. espantarse en ver el fuego. p̃t.º oninix-

mauhti. 99. pararse en la carrera o en el camino. p̃t.º

oninotilquetz. 100. recular o boluer atras. pret.º oni-

valtzinquiz. onivaltziniloth. 1. prouar a hazer algo.

p̃t.º onitlayeheco. 2. esforçarse pa hazer algo. o poner

todas las fuerças pa hazer algo. p̃t.º yxquich onicahan.

3. arrojarse con impeto pa hazer algo. o darse todo

a vna cosa. p̃t.º yc oninomotlac. onicnomacac. 4. en

ningũa manera. 5. osar o atreuerse. p̃t.º oninotlapalo.

6. saltar atras. p̃t.º onivaltzincholo. onitzincholo. 7. no

puede sufrir la pena o trabajo. p̃t.º amo onõtlayeco.

a.º onoconyeco. 8. a lo mas quatro vezes. 9. cumplir.

o acabar. p̃t.º onontlaquixti. 10. bozear. p̃t.º onitetza-

tzili. 11. ea pues tu. 12. alto sus. 13. de vna vez.

14. hazer violencia a su coraçon. p̃t.º onicualcentlami.

onicuallanqua ỹ noyollo. 15. hazer algo a cierra ojos

por hazerlo sin temor. p̃t.º onixtetẽmotzolo. oninixte-

teppic. 16. no se parar. o no cesar en el camino. o en

   1.   2.   3.

tlayehecoz, yxquich caana, yc momotla, quimomaca
         4.   5.

yn tletl: auh ça avelmotlapalo, in ye no ytech onaci
            6.   7.

totonqui, çan valtzinq'ça valtzincholoa, amo ontlaye-
         8.

coa: ul' nappa. tlahelnappa yn iuh quichiuh ỹ moye-

heco, ça nimã ahuel õmomayauh ỹ tleco: ca çan ye
              9.

vncan tlateneualli ỹ nappa. Auh yn ontlaquixti
        10.

nappa: nimã ye ic yeh contzatzilia ỹ nanavatzin,
        11.

q'lhuique ỹ teteu. Oc tehuatl, oc cuel tehuatl nana-
  12.   13.

oatze, ma yeh cuel. Auh ỹ nanavatzin çan cen ỹ val-
        14.

motlapalo, quivalcentlami, quivallãcua yn iyollo,
  15.   16.

valixtetẽmotzolo: amo tle yc mixmauhti, a.º moqueh-

quetz, amo motilquetz, a.º tzinquiz: çã nimã ommo-
        17.

tlaztiuetz õmomayauhtiuetz ỹ tleco, çan ic cenya:
     18.   19.

nimã ye ic tlatla, cuecuepoca, tzotzoyoca yn inacayo.

49

And when Tecuciztecatl saw that [Nanauatzin] had cast himself into the flames, and was burning, he gathered himself [for the ordeal] and threw himself into the fire. And it is said that an eagle entered the blaze and also burned itself; and for that reason it has dark brown or blackened feathers. Finally a tiger [ocelot] entered; it did not burn itself, but [only] singed itself; and for that reason remained stained black and white. From here was taken the custom of calling men dexterous in war *quauhtlocelotl*. And they said *quauhtli* first, because the eagle first entered the flames. And last *ocelotl* is said, because the tiger [ocelot] entered the fire after the eagle. After both [the gods] had thrown themselves into the fire, and after they had burned, then the gods seated themselves to wait [to see] from what direction Nanaua[tzin] would come to rise.

que se avia echado en el fuego y ardia, arremetio y echose en el fuego. Y dizque luego vna aguila entro en el fuego y tambien se quemo: y por esso tiene las plumas hoscas o negrestinas. A la postre entro vn tigre no se quemo sino chamascose: y por esso q̃do manchado de negro y blanco. Deste lugar se tomo la costumbre de llamar a los hombres diestros en la guerra quauhtlocelotl. Y dizen primero quauhtli porque el aguila p'mero entro en el fuego. Y dizese a la postre ocelotl porque el tigre entro en el fuego a la postre del aguila. Despues que ambos se ouieron arrojado en el fuego, y despues que se ouierõ quemado: luego los dioses se sentaron a esperar a que pte vendria salir el nanaoa. Despues que estuuiero grã rato esperando,

Auh yn iquac oquittac tecuciztecatl ỹ ye tlatla, quin-

iquac çatepã ypã õmomayauh, nimã ye no ic tlatla.

20.

Auh yn iuh conitoa, quilmach nimã no ic onevac yn

21.   22.

quauhtli quimontoquili, õmotlaztiuetz yn tleco, õmo-

24.

tlecomayauh, oc yehvatl no uellalac ypampan yviyo

23.   25.   26.

cuicheuac, cuichectic: auh ça ontlatzacui yn ocelotl,

27.

aocmo cenca vellala yn tletl vetzito, yc ça motlecui-

28.

cuilo, motletlecuicuilo, motlechichino, aocmo cenca

29.   [40.]

vellalac, ypampan çan cuicuiltic,[22] motlilchachapani,

[41.]

motlilchachapatz. Jn hin quilmach vncan man,

vncan mocuic yn tlatolli, ynic ytolo, tenevalo yn

[42.]

aquin tiacauh oquichtli quauhtlocelotl tocayotilo:

[43.]

yeh yacattiuh yn quauhtli mitoa, q'l ypampa yn

[45.]

onteyacan tleco, auh ça ontlatzacuia yn ocelotl ynic

[46.]

mocẽcamaytoa q̃uhtlocelotl, ypampa ỹ çatepan on-

vetz tleco. Auh yn ye iuhqui yn omextin õmomama-

[47.]

yauhque tleco, yn iquac ye otlatlaque. Nimã yc qui-

[48.]

chixtimotecaque yn teteu yn campa yeh q'çaquiuh

nanauatzin yn achto onvetz tleco ynic tonaz ynic

[49.]   [50.]

tlathui. Yn iquac ye vecauhtica onoque, mochixca-

la carrera. p̃t.º amo oninoquehquetz, amo oninotil-

quetz. 17. Yr de vna vez. p̃. yc cen oniya. 18. estallar

o respendar. p̃t.º ocuecuepocac. 19. rechinar. pret.º

otzotzoyocac.

20. partirse para yr a alguna pte. p̃t.º ononeuh. onon-

evac. 21. Seguir a otro. p̃t.º onocontoq'li. 22. arrojarse

en el fuego. pret.º ononnotlecomayauh. 23. cosa hosca.

o negrestina. 24. pluma. ca.º noviyo. 25. Yr despues

o a la postre. p̃t.º onontlatzacui. 26. tigre. caso. noce-

louh. 27. mancharse del fuego. p̃t.º oninotlecuicuilo.

oninotletlecuicuilo. 28. chamuscarse. p̃t.º oninotle-

chichino. 29. cosa mãchada. 40. Salpicar de tinta. o

de negro. p̃t.º oninotlilchachapani. oninotlilchacha-

patz. 41. tomarse. p̃t.º oman. omocuic. 42. hombre

diestro en las armas. 43. Yr delãte. p̃t.º oniyacatia.

45. guiar. p̃t.º oniteyacan. 46. dezirse en vna palabra

quauhtlocelotl. caso Noquauh. nocelouh. 47. sentarse

a esperar. p̃t.º onicchixtimotlali. onicchixtimotecac.

48. de donde o de que pte. 49. distancia de tp̃o.

50. estar esperando. p̃t.º oninochixcacatca. oninochix-

caonoca.

---

22. Numbering in the text and references is confused in the original. No. 44 is skipped in both columns. Numbers are indistinct. To correspond with the numbering in the column of notes, we skip from 29 to 40 in the Aztec column.

After they had waited a long time, the heavens began to redden, and in every quarter the dawn appeared. And they say that after this the gods knelt down to wait [to see] where Nanaua[tzin], become sun, would rise. In every direction they looked, turning about. They never succeeded in guessing or saying from what quarter he would rise. They agreed in nothing. Some thought that he would come up in the north, and stood up to look there. Others stood to look toward the west; others to the south. They conjectured that he was to come forth in all directions, because at all the cardinal points there was the brilliance of the dawn. Others placed themselves so as to look to the east. They said: "Here, from this direction, the sun must rise." The declaration of these was true. They say that those who looked to the east were Quetzalcoatl; a second named Ehecatl; and another named Totec, or, by another name Anauatl itecu, and by [still] another name, Tlatlauic Tezcatlipoca; and others called Mimixcoa, who are without number; and four women, one named Tiacapan, another Teicu, a third Tlacoyeua, and a fourth Xocoyotl.

Començose a parar colorado el cielo: y en toda pte aparecio la luz d'l alua. Y dizen que despues desto, los dioses se hincaron de rodillas pa esperar adonde saldria nanava hecho sol, a todas ptes mirauan boluiendose en rededor, nun acertaron a pensar ni a dezir a que pte saldria, en ninguna cosa se determinaron. Algunos pensaron que saldria de la pte del norte y paronse a mirar hazia alla: otros se pararon a mirar hazia el poniente: otros hazia el medio dia: a todas ptes suspecharon que avia de salir, porque a todas ptes avia resplandor del alua: otros se pusieron a mirar hazia el oriente dixeron aqui desta pte a de salir el sol: el dho destos fue verdadero. dizen que los que miraron hazia el oriente fueron Quetzalcoatl el 2.° que llama hecatl y otro que se llama totec y por otro nõbre anavatl ytecu y por otro nombre tlatlauic tezcatlipuca: y otros que se llamã mimixcoa que son inumerables: y quatro mugeres, la vna se llama tiacapã, la otra teycu, la tercera tlahcoyeua, la quarta xocoyotl.

onoque teteu, niman ye yc peua yn tlachichiliui novi-

53.   54.   55.

yãpa tlayaualo yn tlauizcalli, yn tlatlauillotl: yn iuh

56.

conitoa nimã ye ic motlanquaquetza yn teteu ynic

quichiezque yncampa yeh quiçaq'uh tonatiuh omo-

57.   58.   59.

chiuh, noviyampa tlachixque, ahuicpa tlachie, moma-

60.   61.

lacachotinemi: ahcã vel centetix yn intlatol yn

62.   63.   64.

innemachiliz, atle y vel yaca yn quitoque. Cequintin

65.   66.   67.

momatque, ca mictlãpa ỹ quiçaquiuh yc vmpa ytzti-

68.   69.

momanque: cequĩtin civatlampa cequintin vitz-

70.

tlampa ytztimomanque, nouiyampa motemachique

ypampa ỹ çan tlayavalo tlatlavillotl. Auh yn cequin-

71.

tin vel vmpa ytztomomanque ỹ tlauhcopa, quitoque

72.

Ca yeh vmpa hin ye vncan hin yn quiçaquiuh tona-

73.

tiuh: yehuantin vel neltic yn intlatol yn vmpa

74.

tlachixque yn vmpa mapiloque. Yuh q'toa yehuantin

yn vmpa tlachixq quetzalcoatl yc ontetl ytoca hecatl,

yoã yn totec, anoço anavatl ytecu, yoan tlatlavic tez-

catlipuca, no yehuantin yn moteneua mimixcoa ỹ

amo çã tlapoaltin, yoã ciua navin tiacapan, teycu,

tlahcoyeua, xocoyotl. Auh yn iquac oquiçaco yn

51. pararse colorado. p̃t.º otlachichiliuh. 52. por todas ptes. 53. ponerse en rededor o rodear. p̃t.º otlayaualo. 54. el alua del dia. caso. notlauizcal. 55. claridad. caso. notlatlavillouh. 56. hincar las rodillas en tierra. p̃t.º oninotlanquaquetz. 57. por todas ptes. 58. mirar. p̃t.º onitlachix. 59. boluerse al rededor. p̃t.º oninomala-cacho. 60. de ninguna manera. o en nĩgun lugar. 61. adunarse. o concertarse. p̃t.º ocentetix. 62. pen-samj.º ca. nonemachiliz. 63. cosa no determinada. 64. algunos. 65. pensar. p̃t.º oninoma. oninomat. 66. hazia el norte. 67. ponerse a mirar. p̃. onitztimo-quetz. 68. hazia el poniente. 69. hazia el medio dia. 70. esperar. p̃t.º oninotemachi. 71. hazia el oriĕte. 72. en aquel lugar. o en este lugar. 73. verificarse. p̃t.º oneltic. 74. señalar con el dedo. p̃t.º onimapilo.

And when the sun came to rise, he looked very red. He appeared to waddle from one side to the other. None could look at him, because he snatched sight from the eyes. He shone and cast rays [of light] from himself in grand style. His light and his rays he poured forth in all directions. And thereafter the moon rose, in the same quarter, the east, like the sun. First the sun came forth, and after him came out the moon; in the order that they entered the fire, in [that] same [order] they came out made sun and moon. And those who tell stories or tales say that they had equal light with which they illuminated [the world]. And when the gods saw that they shed equal brilliance, they again spoke among themselves, and said: "O gods, how shall this be? Will it be well that both go alike? Will it be well that they illuminate equally?" And the gods gave a command, and said: "Let it be thus; let it be thus done." And then one of them went running and with a rabbit struck Tecuciztecatl in the face. He darkened his face and deadened [its] brilliance, and his face remained as it is today.

After both had come forth over the earth, the sun and moon remained still, without moving from one

Y quando vino a salir el sol, parecio muy colorado, parecia que se cõtoneava de vna pte a otra, nadie lo pudia mirar porque quitaua la vista de los ojos, resplandecia y echava rayos de si en grã manera su luz y sus rayos se derramo por todas ptes. Y despues salio la lũa en la misma pte del oriente a par del sol: Primero salio el sol y tras el salio la luna, por la orden que entraron en el fuego por la mesma salierõ hechos sol y luna. Y dizen los q̃ cuẽtan fabulas o hablillas que tenian ygual luz con que alumbrauan y desque vieron los dioses que ygualmente resplandecian, hablaronse otra vez y dixeron. O dioses como sera esto? sera bien que vayan ambos a la par? sera bien que ygualmente alumbren? Y los dioses dieron sñia y dixeron. Sea desta manera, hagase desta manera. Y luego vno dellos fue corriendo y dio con vn conejo en la cara a tecuciztecatl escureciole la cara y amatole el resplandor y quedo como agora esta su cara. Despues que ouieron salido ambos sobre la tr̃a,

estuuieron quedos sin mudarse de vn lugar sol y la luna. Y los dioses otra vez se hablaron y dixeron.

omomanaco tonatiuh, yuhquin tlapalli monenecuilo-
76.   77.   78.
timani, amo vel yxnamico, teyxmimicti, cenca tlanex-
79.
tia motonameyotia, yn itonameyo noviyampa aaciti-
80.
moquetz, auh yn itonalmiyo noviyampa cacalac:
81.
Auh çatepan quiçaco ỹ tecuciztecatl quivaltocatia çan
82.   83.
ye no vmpa ỹ tlauhcopa ytloc õmomanaco yn tona-

tiuh: yn iuh ơnvetzque tleco, çan no yuh valquizque,

valmotocatiaque. Auh yn iuh conitoa tlâtlanonotza,
84.   85.   86.
teçaçaçanilhuia çan nêneuhqui yn intlachieliz mo-

chiuh, ynic tlanextiaya: yn iquac oquimittaque teteu

ỹ çan nêneuhqui yntlachieliz, niman ye no ceppa yc
87.
nenonutzalo, q̃toque. Quen yezque hin, teteuhe? cuix
88.   89.
onteixtin otlatocazque, onteixtī yuh tlanextizque?
90.
Auh ỹ teteu muchintin vallatzontecque, quitoque.
91.
Juh yez hin, yuh muchiuaz hin? Niman yc ce tlacatl
92.   93.
õmotlalotiquiz ỹ teteu, yc conixviuitequito yn tochin
94.
in yehuatl tecuciztecatl, yc conixpopoloque, yc con-
95.
ixômictique yn iuhqui axcan yc tlachie. Auh yn ye

iuhqui yn iquac yc omomanaco onteyxtin, ye no

75. reboluerse a vna pte y a otra. p̃t.º oninonenecuilo.

76. no es posible. 77. mirar en la cara. p̃t.º oniquixna-
mic. 78. quitar la vista de los ojos. p̃t.º oteixmimicti.

79. dilatarse. p̃t.º oacitimoquetz. 80. ẽtrar por todas
ptes. p̃. ocacalac. 81. seguir a otro. p̃. onictocatia.

82. en el mismo lugar. 83. cabe el o con el. ca.º notloc.

84. dezir hablillas a otro. p̃t.º oniteçaçanilhui. onitla-
nonotz. 85. cosa ygual a otra. 86. aparencia o gesto.

ca. notlachieliz. notlachixca. notlachieya. 87. como
sera esto? 88. dos iuntos. 89. andar camino. p̃. onotla-
tocac. 90. dar sentencia. p̃. onitlatzontec. 91. desta

manera se hara esto. 92. hujr. p̃. oninotlalotiquiz.

93. herir en la cara. p̃. oniteixhuitec. 94. estragar
la cara a algun. p̃. oniteixpopolo. 95. afear la cara

a otro. p̃. oniteixmicti.

96.   97.
cueleh ahuel olini, ahuel otlatoca, çan momanque,
98.
motetẽmanque: yc ye no ceppa quitoque ỹ teteu,

96. no puede. 97. mouerse. p̃. onolin. oninolini.

98. pararse con firmo pposito de no mouerse mas.

place. And the gods once more spoke, and said: "How may we live? The sun does not move himself! Are we to live among the peasants? Let us all die and make him revive through our death!" And then the Wind took charge of killing all the gods, and he slew them. And it is told that one, named Xolotl, refused to die, and said to the gods: "O gods, let me not die." And he wept exceedingly, so that his eyes swelled with weeping. And when the slayer came to him, he hid in the maize fields, and he changed and turned himself into the foot of a maize plant which has two stalks, and the field workers call it *xolotl*. And he was seen and found among the feet of the maize stalks. Again he took flight and hid among the maguey plants, and changed himself into a maguey plant which has two bodies, which is called *mexolotl*. Once more he was seen, and he took flight and placed himself in the water and made himself into a fish which is called *axolotl*. From there they took him and slew him. And they say that although the gods were slain, not on that account did the sun move. And then the Wind began to blow and raise a strong gale. He made him move, so that he might go on his way. And after the sun began to travel, the moon was quiet in the place where he was.

Como podemos biuir no se menea el sol, emos d' biuir entre los villanos? muramos todos y hagamosle q̃ resucite por nr̃a muerte. Y luego ayre se encargo de matar a todos los dioses, y matolos. Y dizese que vno llamado Xolotl rehusava la muerte, y dixo a los dioses. O dioses no muera yo y lloraua gran manera de manera que se le hincharon los ojos de llorar. Y quando llego a el el q̃ mataua hecho a huyr, ascondiose entre los mayzales, y boluiose y con[ver]tiose en pie de mayz q̃ tiene dos cañas y los labradores le llaman xolotl. Y fue visto y hallado entre los pies del mayz, otra vez hecho a huyr y se escondio entre los magueys y convertiose en maguey que tiene dos cuerpos, q̃ se llama mexolotl: otra vez fue visto y hecho a huyr y metiose en el agua y hizose pez q̃ se llama axolotl de alla le tomaron y le mataron. Y dizen que avnque fueron muertos los dioses no por esso se mouio el sol y luego el viento començo a suflar o ventear reziamente: el le hizo mouerse pa que anduuiese su camino. Y despues q̃ el sol començo a caminar, la lũa se estuuo queda en el lugar donde estaua.

56

qntinemizque amo olini yn tonatiuh cuix tiquineloti-

100.

nemizq y maceualti: auh yn hin matoca mozcalti, ma

timuchintin timiquica. Nimã yc yeh ytequiuh õmo-

chiuh yn hecatl ye quimictia yn teteu: auh yn iuh

1.

conitoa y xolotl ah momiquitlania, q'milhui y teteu.

2.

Macamo nimiqui teteuhe. Jc cẽca chocaya, vel yxpo-

3.

poçavac, yxquatolpopoçauac: auh in ye itech onaci

4.   5.   6.

miquiztli, çan teixpampa yeuac, cholo, toctitlan calac-

7.

tiuetz ypan õmixeuh, yc omocueptiuetz yn toctli ome

8.

mani, maxaltic yn quitocayotia millaca xolotl. Auh

vncan yttoc yn toctitlan, ye no ceppa teixpampa

9.

yeuac, ye no cuele metitlan calactiuetz, no yc õmo-

cueptiuetz y metl ome mani yn itoca mexolotl. Ye

no ceppa yttoc, ye no cuele atlan calactiuetz axolotl

mocuepato ye vel vmpa canato ynic cõmictique. Auh

quitoa y manel muchintin teteu õmicque, ça nel amo

vel yc olin amo vel yc otlatocac y teutl tonatiuh yc

ytequiuh õmochiuh y ehecatl, moquetz yn ehecatl,

10.   11.   12.

cenca molhui, totocac yn ehecac, quin yehuatl vel

13.

colini, niman ye ic otlatoca. Auh y iqc ye otlatoca,

14.

çan vmpa ommocauh y metztli: quiniquac yn ocal-

15.   16.

aquito ycalaquian tonatiuh, ye no cuele yc valeuac

17.   18.

y metztli: yc vncã mopatilique, motlallotique ynic

19.

ceceppa valquiça, tlacemilhuitiltia yn tonatiuh, auh

omotetẽma. oninoteteuhtlali. oninoteteuhquetz. 99. mezclarse con otros. p̃. onitenelo. 100. resucitar con ayuda de alguno. o murir porque solamẽte biua otro. p̃. teca oninozcalti. 1. rehusar la muerta. p̃. aonino-miquitlan. amo oninomiquitlan. 2. hincharse los ojos. p̃. onixpopoçauac. 3. hincharse los parpados de los ojos. p̃. onixquatolpopoçauac. onixquatoleeuac. onixeeuac. 4. huyr de alguno. p̃. oteixpampaneuac. onicholo. 5. entre mayz verde. 6. ẽtrar de presto o subitamente. p̃. onicalactivetz. 7. conuertirse. o tomar figura de otra cosa. p̃. ypan oninixeuh. ypã onino-cuep. yc oninocuep. 8. cosa doblada. o cosa q̃ esta de dos en dos en vna rayz. 9. entre los magueys. 10. poner conato o fuerça. pa hazer aglo. p̃t.º oninol-hui. 11. hazer algo con vehemẽcia. p̃. onitotocac. 12. ventear. pret.º oehecac. 13. mouer algo. p̃. onic-olini. 14. quedarse en alguna parte. p̃. oninocauh. onõ-nocauh. 15. su entrada del sol o el poniente. caso. nocalaquian. 16. partirse de algun lugar. pret.º onon-euac. ononeuh. 17. pasar vno a otro. yendo por otro camino. p̃. onicpatili. 18. apartarse vna cosa de otra. p̃. onictlalloti. 19. durar vn dia. p̃. onitlacemilhuitilti. 20. el trabajo de la noche sustentar. o sufrir. pret.º onictlaz. 21. trabaiar de noche. pret.º oniyoualtequit.

After the sun had set, the moon began to move. Thus the one got away from the other. And thus they come forth at different times. The sun endureth one day, and the moon worketh at night (or illumineth at night). From this cometh what is said: that Tecuciztecatl would have been the sun if he had cast himself first into the fire, because he was named first, and offered precious things in his penance.

Eclipse of the Moon.

When the moon is eclipsed, he becometh almost dark; he becometh blackened; he turneth a dark brown. Then the earth darkeneth. When this cometh to pass, women with child feared miscarriage. A great dread seized them that that which they had in their bodies would become mice. And as a remedy for this they took a piece of obsidian in the mouth or they placed it in the girdle over the belly and [did so] in order that the children [whom they carried] in the womb would not be born lipless or noseless or wry-mouthed, or cross-eyed, or that [one] might not be born monstrous.

The people of Xaltocan held the moon as a god and made him special offerings and sacrifices.

Despues que el sol se puso començo la luna a andar: desta manera se desuiaron el vno del otro: y ansi salen ẽ diuersos tiempos. El sol dura vn dia y la luna trabaia en la noche o alumbra en la noche. De aqui parece lo que se dize q̃ el tecuciztecatl avia de ser sol si p'mero se ouiera echado en el fuego porque el p'mero fue nõbrado y ofrecio cosas preciosas en su pñia.

Quando la luna se eclipsa, parase casi oscura, ennegrecese, parase hosca: luego se escurese la tierra. Quando esto aconteçe las preñadas temian de abortar, tomauales gran temor que lo q̃ tenian en el cuerpo se a de boluer raton. Y para remedio desto tomavan vn pedaço de ytztli ẽ la boca o ponianle en la çintura sobre el vientre y para que los ninos que en el vientre no saliesen sin beços o sin narizes, o boquituertos, o bizgos: o porq̃ no naciese monstro.

Los de xaltoca tenian por dios a la luna y le hazia particulares ofrendas y sacrificios.

20. 21.
ỹ metztli yovaltequitl quitlaça, ceyoval quitlaça yo-
valtequiti. Jc vncan hin neci, mitoa ca yehuatl tonatiuh yezquia ỹ metztli tecuciztecatl yntla yeh achto
onvetzini tleco, ypampa ca yehuatl achto mixquetz
ynic muchi tlaçotli ypan tlamaceuh.—Nican tlami
ynhin nenonotzalli, çaçanilli, in ye vecauh yc tlâtla-
nonutzaya veuetque, yn impiel catca.

Metztli qualo.

1. 2.
Jn iquac qualo metztli, yxtlileua yxcuicheua. cuich-
3.
euatimomana. tlayouatimomana. Yn iquac hĩ mu-
4. 5. 6.
chiua, vel motẽmatia yn ootzti, tlaueimatia, momauh-
7. 8.
tiaya ma nelli moquimichcuepti, ma quiquimichti-
9.
mocuepti yn impilhuan. Auh ynic quĩtẽmatia, ynic
10. 11.
mopahtiaya, ynic amo yuhqui ympan muchiuaz,
12. 13. 14.
ytztli yncamac, anoço ỹxillan quitlaliaya. ypampa
15.
ynic amo tencuayuizque tencuatizque ympilhuã,
16. 17.
anoço yacaquatizque, yacacotonizque, anoço tẽpatzi-
18.
uizque, tennecuiliuizque. yxpatziuizque, yxnecuili-
19.
uizque, yxvacaliuizque, yn anoço atlacacemelle tlacatiz. yn amo tlacamelavac.

In hin metztli yehoan quimoteutiaya ỹ xaltocameca,
quitlamaniliaya, quimaviztiliaya.

1. pararse negrestino. p̃. onixtlileuac. onixcuicheuac.
2. pararse como ahumado. p̃. onicuicheuac. onipuch-
euac. 3. hazerse tinieblas. o oscuridad. p̃t. otlayouac.
otlayouatimomã. 4. aver miedo q̃ le venga algũ mal.
p̃. oninotẽma. onitlatẽma. 5. hembra preñada. ca.
notzecauh. 6. temer el peligro del pto. p̃. onitlaueima
oninomauhti. 7. por ventura. 8. boluerse ratõ. p̃.
oninoquimichcuep. 9. temer asi algun mal o a otro.
p̃. onictẽma. onictlatẽmachili. 10. Remediar. p̃. onino-
pahti. 11. acõtecer. p̃. nopan omochiuh. 12. Nauaja
d' piedra. caso. nitz. 13. en la boca. ca. nocamac.
14. la varriga. ca. noxillan. 15. Nacer falto de los
beços. p̃. onitẽquayuh. onitẽquatix. quatic. 16. Nazer
falto de las narizes. p̃. oniyacaquatix. quatic. oniya-
cacoton. 17. Nacer boquituerto. p̃. onitẽpatziuh. oni-

59

Third Chapter, of the Stars Called Castor and Pollux.

These people paid particular reverence and [made] special sacrifices to Castor and Pollux, in the sky, which move near the Pleiades, which are in the sign of Taurus. They made these sacrifices and ceremonies when [the stars] newly appeared to the east after sunset. After having offered incense, they said: "Now [hath] Yoaltecutli come forth, and Yacauiztli. What will come to pass this night? Or what end will the night have—fortunate or adverse?" Three times they offered incense (and [this] must be because they are three stars), the first time at the first quarter of the night, another time at ten, and the third [time] when it beginneth to be morning.—They name these stars *mamalhuaztli,* and by that same name they call the sticks with which they drill a fire; because it seemeth to them that they somewhat resemble [the stars] and that from them there came to them this manner of producing fire. From this it was customary that the

Hazia esta gente particular reuerencia y particulares sacrificios a los mastelexos del cielo q̃ andã cerca de las cabrillas que es en el signo del toro. hazian estos sacrificios y cerimonias q̃ñ nueuamente parecia por el oriente despues de la puesta del sol. Despues de auer ofrecidole encienso, dezian ya salido youaltecutli y yacauiztli, que acontecera esta noche o que fin abra la noche prospero o aduerso. Tres vezes ofrecian encienso y deue ser porque ellas son tres estrellas. la vna vez a p'ma noche. la otra vez a hora de las diez. la 3.ª quando comiença amanecer.—llaman a estas estrellas mamalhuaztli y por este mismo nõbre llaman a los palos con q̃ sacan lumbre porq̃ les parece q̃ tienen alguna semeiança cõ ellas y que de alli les vino esta manera de sacar fuego. De aqui tomaron por costumbre de hazer vnas quemaduras en la moñeca los varones a honrra de aq̃llas estrellas. Dezian que el q̃ no fuese señalado de aquellas que-

tẽnecuiliuh. tempatiliuh. 18. Nacer bizgo. p̃. onixpa-
tziuh. õixnecuiliuh. vacaliuh. 19. nacer monstro.

Capitulo tercero de las estrellas llamadas mas-
telejos

1. Mamalhuaztli.

Yn iquac valneci, valmotema tlenamacoya. tlato-
2.
toniloya. yc mitoaya, ovalhuetz in yoaltecutli, in
yacauiztli: quen vetziz in youalli quen tlathuiz. Auh
yn hin tlenamacoya expa ỹ muchiuaya, yq̃c yn
3.   4.   5.
tlapoyava, tlaquauhtlapoyaua, yoan netetequizpã,
6.   7.   8.
tlatlapitzalizpan, yquac hin neçoaya neuitzmanaloya:
9.   10.
yc expa tlenamacoya, yquac yn tlavizcalleua, tlauiz-
11.   12.
calli moq̃tzȧ, yn tlatlalchipaua, yn ye tlathuinavac.
13.
Auh ynic mitoa mamalhuaztli, ytech moneneuilia yn
14.   15.   16.
tlequavitl: yehica yn iquac tlequauhtlaxo, ca moma-
17. 18.   19.   20.
mali yn tlequavitl, ynic vetzi, ỹyc xotla, ynic mopitza
21.
tletl. No yoan ynic nematlatiloya, ynic momatlatiaya
22.   23.
toquichti, yehoatl quimacacia, mimacacia, ymaca-
24.
xoya, mitoaya quilmach yn aq'n amo nematlatile,
25.
ymac tlequauhtlaxoz ỹ mictlan yn iquac omic.

Yehica yn toquichti muchi tlacatl momatlatiaya,
26. 27.   [28.]
nenecoc ynmac quiuiuipanaya, quitetecpanaya yn
[29.]   [30.]
innematlatil: yc quitlayehecalhuiaya yn mamalhuaz-

1. Las estrellas que se llaman mastelexos. 2. este
es el nombre de aquellas estrellas. 3. p'ma noche.
escurecerse la noche. p̃. otlapoyauac. 4. mucho. o
rezio. 5. la hora de echarse a dormir. ca. nonetequiz-
pan. 6. la hora de tocar las bozinas. ca. notlapitza-
lizpã. 7. la hora de ofrecer sangre de las orejas. 8. la
hora de ofrecer puntas de maguey ensangrentadas.
9. asumar el alua. p̃. otlauizcalleuac. 10. quando el
alua esta ya bien demostrado. p̃. otlauizcalli moquetz.
11. parecerse la tierra con la luz del alua ya muy clara.
p̃. otlatlalchipauac. 12. ante de amanecer. o junto al
alua. 13. comparse. o semejarse. pre. onitlaneneuili.
onitlaneuiuili. 14. instrumẽto de palo pa sacar fuego.
ca. notlequauh. 15. sacar fuego cõ aquel instrum.^to p̃.
onitlequauhtlaz. 16. barrenarse. p̃. oninomamal. 17.
con que. 18. salir. p̃. ouetz. 19. brotar. p̃. oxotlac.
20. encenderse. p̃. omopitz. 21. quemar la moneca en
vnas ptes. p̃. oninomatlati. 22. temer a otro. p̃. oni-

61

men make certain burns on the wrist in honor of those stars. They said of him who was not marked by those burns that, when he died, there in hell they would produce fire on his wrist, drilling it as those do who here drill fire with the stick.

maduras quando se muriese q̃ alla en el infierno avian de sacar el fuego de su moñeca barrenãdola como qñ aca sacã el fuego del palo.

The star Venus these people named Citlalpol or Uey citlalin, and they said that when it riseth in the east it maketh four assaults. The [first] three times it shineth little and hideth again; and at the fourth it cometh forth with all its brightness and followeth its course. And they say of its light that it is like that of the moon. On its first assault they held it an omen of evil, saying that it brought sickness with it. And therefore they shut the doors and windows so that its light might not come in. And sometimes they took it as a good omen. And at the beginning of the time that it started to appear to the east, they slew captive men in reverence to it, and offered it their blood, spattering it toward [the star] with their fingers.

A la estrella de venus la llamaua esta gente citlal-pul, vey citlalli y dezian que quando sale por el oriente haze quatro aremetidas, y a las tres luze poco y bueluese a asconder: y a la quarta sale con toda su claridad y procede por su curso. y dizen de su luz que parece a la de la luna. En primera arremetida teni-anla de mal aguero diziendo que traya enfermedad consigo, y por esto cerrauan las puertas y ventanas porq̃ no entrase su luz. Y a las vezes la tomavan por buen aguero. Y al p'ncipio de t͠po que començaua a aparecer por el oriente matauan hõbres captiuos por su reuerencia, y ofrecianle la sangre salpicando hazia ella con los dedos.

tli, ỹ iuh vipãtoc, tecpantoc, no yuh q'uiuipanaya,

quitetecpanaya yn ĩmac ynnematlatil.

1. **Citlalpul.**

Vey citlalin.

2.

Mitoa yn iquac yancuican valcholoa, valquiça nappã

3.   4.   5.

poliui, popoliuhtiuetzi: auh çatepan vel cueponi cue-

6.   7.

pontimotlalia, cuepontica, tlanextitica yuhquin metz-

tona yc tlanextia. Auh yn iquac yancuican valcholoa,

8.   9.

cenca maviztli motecaya, nemauhtiloya, noviyan

10.   11.

motzatzacuaya yn tlecalli yn puchquiavatl, mitoaya

12.   13.   14.   15.

aço cocolizço ytla ahqualli quitquitiuitz yn oq'çaco:

16.   17.   18.

auh yn quẽman quiqualittaya. Auh no micoaya yn

19.   20.

iãc valcholoa, yzcaltiloya, quitlaqualiaya ymezçotica

21.   22.

ỹ mamalti: contlatzitzicuiniliaya, contlatlatlaxiliaya.

23.

contlayyauiliaya.

quimacaz. 23. temerse. p̃. omimacaz. oymacaxoc. 24.

el q̃ no tiene aquestas quemaduras ẽ la moneca. 25.

infierno. 26. de ambas ptes. 27. mano o moneca. ca.

nomac. 28. ordenar en rencle. p̃. onicviuipan. onicte-

tecpan. 29. quemadura de la moneca. ca. nonema-

tlatil. 30. ymitar. o remedar. o arentar. p̃. onictlaye-

hecalhui. 31. estar alguna cosa puesta en rencle.

1. el luzero de la mañana. 2. saltar. o arremeter. o

huyr. p̃. onicholo. 3. desaparecerse. pre. onipoliuh.

4. a la postre. 5. salir. la estrella. o brotar. o reuẽtar.

pre. onicuepon. onicuepontimotlali. onicueponti-

catca. onitlanextiticatca. 6. ansi como. 7. esplandecer

la luna. p̃. ometztonac. 8. imprimir temor. o espanto.

p̃. mauiztli omotecac. 9. en todo lugar. 10. encerrarse.

pre. oninotzatzacu. 11. humero. ca. notlecal. nopuch-

quiauauh. 12. cosa enferma. o que cavsa d' enferme-

dad. 13. algo. 14. cosa mala. o cosa dañosa. 15.

trayer. aca. p̃. oniquitquitza. oniquitq'tiuitza. 16.

algũas vezes. 17. cosa buena. 18. murir. o matar.

p̃. omicoac. 19. mantẽñer. o cevar. p̃. oizcalti-

loc. 20. ruziar con sangre a los ydolos. p̃. onictlaquali.

21. ruziar con sangre, con el golpe del dedo medio

resoltido sobRe el pulgar. p̃. onitlatzitzicuini. 22.

arrojar por modo de ofrenda. p̃. onitlatlatlaz. 23. alçar

Fourth Chapter.

The comet these people called *citlalin popoca,* which meaneth smoking star. They held it as a prognostication of the death of some prince or a king, or of war, or of hunger. The common folk said: "This is our hunger."

Llamaua esta gente a la cometa. citlalin popuca que q. d. estrella que humea: tenianla por prenostico de la muerte de algun principe o rey, o de guerra, o de hambre. La gente vulgar dezia, esta es nr̃a hambre.

The flaming [tail] of the comet these people called *citlalin tlamina,* which meaneth, the star casteth a dart. And they said that that dart always fell upon something living—a hare, or a rabbit, or some other animal; and wheresoever it would go, a worm was then formed. Wherefore that animal was not to be

A la inflamacion de la cometa, llamaua esta gente citlalin tlamina que q. d. la estrella tira saeta y dezian que siempre q̃ aquella saeta. caya sobre algũa cosa biua liebre o conejo o otro animal, y donde yria luego se criaua vn gusano. PoR lo qual aquel animal no era de comer. Por esta causa procuraua esta gente de

algo en reuerencia del que esta lexos ofreciendoselo. Y tambien q. d. alçar el pie o la mano andando haziendo areyte o dança. Tambien q. d. yrse presto a algun lugar, o estar poco en el. Y para alçar otra cosa no se vsa. pre. onitlaiyauh. oniniyauh. onõniyavato.

Capitulo quarto

1. **Citlalin popuca.**

        2.   3.   4.

Mitoaya tlatocatetzauitl. ye tlatocamicoaz, aço aca vey

     5.   6.

tlaçopilli ye miquiz: Yoan no quitoaya aço cana ye

     7.   8.

valmotzacuaz, aço ye oliniz teuatl tlachinolli: yoan

  9.   10.   11.

anoço ye mayanaloz. Quitoaya ỹ macevalti aço tlapiz

hi, aço apiztli q'toa.

1. Cometa. 2. aguero contra los SS. y reyes. 3. murir reyes o SS. 4. por ventura alguno. 5. persona de noble linaje. 6. por uentura en alguna pte. 7. reuelarse contra su. s.ᵒʳ p̃. oualmotzacu. 8. leuantarse guerra. p̃. oolĩ yn teuatl tlachinolli. ca. noteuauh. notlachinol. 9. o por uentura. 10. a[ver][23] hambre. p̃. omayanaloc. 11. esta es nr̃a hambre. ca. napiz. noteuciuiliz. napizmiquiliz. nomayanaliz.

1. **Citlalin tlamina.**

        2.   3.   4.

Mitoa amo nenquiça, amo nẽvetzi yn itlaminaliz,

    5.   6.   7.

tlaocuillotia. Auh yn tlamintli mitoa citlalminqui,

  8.   9.   10.   11.

ocuillo, aocmo quallo, mauhcayto, tlaelitto, hihielo,

  12.   13.   14.

tetlaeltia. Auh yn youaltica vel nemalhuilo, neolololo,

1. La inflamacion de la cometa. 2. no pasar en valde. p̃. amo onenquiz. 3. no acontecer en valde. p̃. amo onenvetz. 4. golpe de saeta. o inflamacion. ca. notlaminaliz. 5. dar ocasion q̃ se hagan gusanos. p̃. onitlaocuilloti. 6. cosa herida con saeta. ca. notlamin.

---

23. Cf. Paso y Troncoso, *op. cit.*, Vol. VII, p. 261.

eaten. For this reason these people took pains to cover themselves at night, so that the tail of the comet might not fall upon them.

abrigarse de noche porque la inflamacion de la cometa no cayese sobrellos.

The stars which are in the Little Bear these people call Citlalxonecuilli. They represent them in the shape of an *s*, backwards, [of] seven stars. They say they are by themselves, apart from the others, and that they are brilliant. They call them Citlalxonecuilli because they resemble a certain kind of bread which they make like an *s*, which they call *xonecuilli*, which bread was eaten in all the houses each year on the day named Xochilhuitl.

A las estrellas que estan en la boca de la bozina llama este gente citlalxonecuilli. pintanlas a manera de ese rebuelta siete estrellas, dizen q̃ estan por si aptadas de las otras y que son resplandecientes. llamanles citlalxonecuilli porq̃ tienẽ semejã́ça con cierta manera de pan que hazen a manera de ese al qual llaman xonecuilli, el qual pan se comia en todas las casas vn dia el año q̃ se llama xuchilhuitl.

Those stars which, in some places, are called the Great Bear these people called the Scorpion, because they make the outline of a scorpion[24] or *alacrán*.

Aquellas estrellas q̃ en algunas ptes se llama el carro. esta gente las llama esculpiõ porque tienen figura de esculpion o alacran.

---

24. *Esculpion*. In the original, the *l* may have been changed to *r*.

netlapacholo, nequentilo, netlalpililo. Ymacaxo yn itlaminaliz citlalin.

7. cosa a quien la estrella hirio como cõ saeta. 8. **Cosa gusanienta.** 9. no ser comestible. 10. tener temor de algo. p̄. onicmauhcayttac. 11. tener asco de algo. p̄. onictlaelittac. oniquihix. 12. hazer asco. pre. onitetlaelti. 13. abricarse del frio. o de otra cosa dañosa. p̄. oninomalhui. 14. cobijarse. p̄. oninololo. 15. cubrirse. p̄. oninotlapacho. 16. vestirse con las mantas. p̄. oninoquenti. oninotlãqti. oninotlalpili.

1. Citlalxonecuilli.

Çan yyoca onoc. iyoca neztoc. tlãextitoc. cuecuepocatoc. Auh ynic mitoa citlalxonecuilli ca quineneuilia, vel no yuhqui centlamantli tlachichiualli tlaxcalli, anoço tzoualli, nenecoc, cecentlapal quacoltic, quateuilacachtic. Xochilhuitl ypan, yn quaqualoya noviyan cecencalpan, quitzacutimanca ỹ noviyan techachã nechiuililoya.

1. La boca de bozina del norte. 2. estar por si. p̄. yyoca onoca. 3. estar resplandeciendo. p̄. otlanextitoca. ocuecuepocatoca. 4. cosa hechiza. o compuesta. ca. notlachichiual. 5. pan de mayz. 6. pan de semilla de zenizos. ca. notzoal. 7. de ambas ptes. 8. cosa que tiene los cabos doblados, el vn cabo contrario al otro como es la. S. 9. vna fiesta d' demonios. 10. comerse algo en muchos lugares. 11. en cada casa. 12. en todo lugar. 13. en todas las casas. 14. hazerse algo para si mismo. p̄. onicnochiuili.

1. Citlalcolotl.

Çan no yuhqui quineneuilia, quinamiqui yn itlachieliz tequani colotl cuitlapilcocoltic, mamalacachtic, teteuilacachtic yn icuitlapil. Ypampã yc mitoa citlalcolotl.

1. Aquella constellacion q̃ llaman el carro o el esculpion. 2. Cosa semejante. 3. asemejarse a otra cosa. o parecer a otra cosa. pret.º oquineneuili. oquinamic. 4. la aparẽcia o gesto. o figura. ca. notlachieliz. 5. bestia fiera. 6. cosa q̃ tiene la cola a manera de carauato. 7. cola. o rago. ca. nocuitlapil.

These people attributed the wind to a god whom they named Quetzalcoatl, something like god of the wind. The wind bloweth from the four quarters of the world by command of this god, according to what they said. The first quarter it cometh from is from the east, where they say is the terrestrial paradise which they call Tlalocan. This wind they called Tlalocayotl. It is not a furious gale; when it bloweth, it doth not hinder the canoes from moving on the water. The second wind bloweth from the north, where they say hell is; and hence they name it Mictlampa ehecatl, which meaneth the infernal wind. *In hin uel imacaxo,* etc.: this wind is violent, and therefore they fear it greatly. When it bloweth, canoes cannot go on the water. And all which are on the water come out with all the speed they can [muster] because of fear when it bloweth; for often they are endangered by it. The third wind bloweth from the west, where they said was the abode of the Amazons. They called it Ciuatlampa ehecatl or Ciuatecayotl, which is to say wind which bloweth from where the women abide. This wind is not savage, but it is cold. It maketh one tremble with cold. With this wind, navigation is good. The fourth wind bloweth from the south, and they name it Uitz-

Esta gente atribuia el viento a vn dios q̃ llamauan quetzalcoatl bien asi como dios de los vientos. Sofla el viento de quatro ptes del mundo por mandamiento deste dios segun ellos dezian. De la vna pte viene de hazia el oriente, donde ellos dizen estar el payso terrenal al qual llaman tlalocan. A este viento la llamauan tlalocayotl: no es viento furioso, quando el sofla no impide las canoas andar por el agua. El segundo viento sofla de hazia el norte donde ellos dizen estar el infierno y asi le llaman mictlampa ehecatl que q. d. el viento infernal. Yn hin vel ymacaxo etc. este viento es furioso y por eso le temen mucho quando el sofla no pueden andar las canoas por el agua. Y todos los que andan por el agua se salen por temor qñ el sofla con toda priesa que puedẽ porque muchas vezes peligran con el. El tercero viento sofla de hazia el occidente donde ellos dezian que era la abitacion de las amaçonas llamauanle ciuatlampa ehecatl o ciuatecayotl que q. d. viento que sofla de donde abitan las mugeres. este viento no es furioso: pero es frio, haze templar de frio con este viento bien se nauegan El quarto viento sofla de hazia el medio dia y llamanle vitztlãpa ehecatl q. d. viento q̃ sofla de aquella pte donde fueron los dioses que llaman viuitznava: este viento en estas ptes es furioso,

[1]. **Ehecatl.**

[2.]
Moteneuaya yc quinotzaya quetzalcoatl. Nauhcampã
[3.]   [4.]   [5.]
vallauh. Nauhcampa valitztiuh. Ynic ceccã vallauh
[6.]
vmpa yn iquiçayampa tonatiuh, quitoaya tlalocan.
7.
Ynin ehecatl vmpa vallauh quitocayotiaya tlalocayotl,
8.   9.   10.
amo cẽca temauhti, amo cenca totoca vel ypan acal-
11.   12.   13.   14.
tica viloa, vel ypan quixoa yn atlan, vel ypã panoa.
15.   16.
Ynic occan vallauh moteneua mictlampa, auh yn hin
17.   18.   19.
motocayotia mictlampa ehecatl. Yn hin vel ymacaxo
20.   21.
vellamauhtia, cẽca totoca yn iquac moquetza, amo
22.   23.
vel quixnamiqui ỹ acalli amo vellauilteco, amo vel

tlaxtlapalolo, avel yxtlapal viloa, ahvel tlanecuilolo
24.   25.
yn atlan, çan mauhcaquixoa, mauhcaquiça yn tlapa-
26.   27.
nauique, yn atlaca, ỹ tlatlamaque, yn tlaminque yn

oquittaque ca mictlampa ehecatl yn omoquetz, yc
28.   29.
cenca motẽmati, motequipachoa, vel moteq'mati
30.   31.   32.
ompilcatoque, ompipilcatoque yn tlaneloa, yn tequi-
33.   34.
tlaneloa, vel momaquauhtilia, ynic vel onq'ça, õma-
35.   36
cana atenco, atẽxipalco, achichiyacpã: yuh quitoa ca
37.   38.   39.   40.
miecpa teatlãmictia, quipolactia yn acalli. Ynic excã
41.   42.
vallauh moteneua civatlampa, motocayotia ciuateca-
43.
yotl, ciuatlampa ehecatl, no quitocayotia ce ehecatl,

anoço maçava, ypampan vmpa valitztiuh maçauacã.
44.   45.
Auh yn hin amono cenca totoca yeceh cenca ytztic,

1. viento. 2. de quatro ptes. 3. venir. p̃. oniualla.
4. venir de hazia alguna parte. p̃. oniualitztia. 5. de
la vna pte. 6. tierra de deleytes como el parayso
terrenal. 7. Nombre del viento que sofla del oriente.
8. no es cosa temerosa o espantable. 9. correr con
impetu. p̃. cenca onitotocac. 10. con canoa. 11. Yr.
p̃. oniya. 12. salir. p̃. oniquiz. 13. del agua. 14. pasar.
p̃. onipano. 15. de la 2.ª pte. 16. de hazia el infierno.
o de hazia el norte. 17. llamarse. p̃. oninotocayoti.
18. este. 19. Ser temido. 20. Cosa que haze espanto.
21. soflar. o estar. p̃. oninoquetz. 22. Yr contra otro.
p̃. oniq'xnamic. 23. atrauesar por delante. o yr a la
bolina. p̃. onitlauiltec. onitlaxtlapalo. onitlanecuilo.
24. Salir de alguna pte con miedo. p̃. onimauhcaquiz.
25. remeros. caso. notlapanauicauh. notlanelocauh.
26. los pescadores. caso. natlaca. notlatlamacauh.
27. los que tiran. ca. notlamincauh. 28. recibir pena.
p̃. oninotequipacho. 29. darse priesa a hazer algo. p̃.
oninotequima. onõpilcatoca.[25] 30. hazerse algo sin
cesar. p̃. onompilcatoca. 31. remar. p̃. onitlanelo.
32. darse priesa a remar. p̃. onitequitlanelo. 33. es-
forçar o areziar los braços en el trabaxo. p̃. oninoma-
quauhtili. 34. sacar la canoa a tierra. onicâcan. onoco-
nâcã. ononnâca. 35. la orilla del agua. ca. natenco.

---

25. The word *onõpilcatoca* appears to have been crossed out in the *Escolios*.

tlampa ehecatl, which meaneth wind blowing from that quarter where went the gods whom they call the Uiuitznaua. This wind, in these parts, is violent, dangerous for boating. Such is its fury sometimes that it uprooteth trees and overturneth walls, and raiseth great waves in the water. Canoes which it meeteth in the water it casteth to the bottom or raiseth high. It is savage like the arctic or north [wind].

peligroso pa nauegar, tanta es su furia a algũas vezes que arancan los arboles y trastornan las paredes, y leuanta grandes olas en el agua las canoas que topa en el agua echalas a fundo o las leuanta en alto, esta furioso como el cierço o norte.

46. 47. 48.
vel tececmicti tepineualti, tepineuh, tetetziliuiti, tete-
49.
tzilquixti, tetzitzilquiti. teuiuiyoquilti, tecuecuech-
50.
quiti, tecuecuechmicti, tecuecuechmiquiti, texillã-
51. 52.
quauhtili, teyomotlanquauhtili, tetzonteconeuh. Auh
53.
tel vel ypan quixoa yn atlan, amo temauhti. amo
54. 55.
temauizcuiti. Auh ynic nauhcampa vallauh ehecatl
56. 57.
vmpã vitztlampa, motocayotia vitztlampa ehecatl.

58.
Auh yn hin cenca vel ymacaxo, mimacaci, netẽmacho
59.
aoc tenauatilli. aoc tetlatolti. Ypãpa cenca totoca,

cenca tlamauhtia. Quitoa yn iquac moquetza, vel
60. 61. 62.
quitzineua, quipoztequi yn quavitl yoan quixitinia
63. 64. 65.
yn tepantli, yn tepãçolli, yn xacalli. quehcatoctia yn
66. 67. 68.
tlatzacuilli, ỹ chinancalli. Auh yn vey atl vel colinia,
69. 70. 71.
quiteponaçoa, quipoçonaltia, ca cuecuẽyotia, yuhquin
72. 73.
tetecuicatimani. cocomocatimani: auh yn acalli caaco-

mayaui, caacotlaça, vel no yuhqui, quinamiqui ỹ

mictlãpa ehecatl.

natenxipalco. 36. cerca de la orilla donde llega la

humedad d'l agua. 37. muchas vezes. 38. ahoga. p̃.

oniteatlanmicti. 39. anegar. o sumir en el agua. p̃.

onitepolacti. 40. de la 3.ª pte. 41. region donde abitã

solas mugeres. 42. nombre del viento que sofla del

occidente. 43. nombres del mesmo viento. 44. empero.

45. muy cosa fria. 46. cosa que mata de frio. 47. cosa

que hierta con frio. 48. cosa que haze teritar de frio.

49. cosa q̃ haze templar o tiritar. 50. cosa que causa

dolor en la barriga. 51. cosa que causa dolor en los

costados. 52. cosa que causa dolor en la cabeça. 53. no

es temerosa. 54. no. Cosa que imprime temor, o

espanto. 55. Y de la quarta pte. 56. la pte del medio

dia. 57. el viento q̃ sofla de la pte del medio dia.

58. temer que le venga algun daño. p̃. oninotẽma.

oninotẽmat. 59. quitar la habla con temor. 60. boluer-

lo de arriba abaxo. o trastornaR algo. p̃. onictzineuh.

61. quebrar cosa de madera o piedra. o metal. p̃. onic-

puztec. 62. derrocar. o desbaratar. p̃. onicxitini. onic-

xini. 63. pared. ca. notepan. 64. casa de paja. ca.

noxacal. 65. lleuar el uiento. p̃. oniquecatocti. 66. Seto

de cañas o de otra cosa. ca. notlatzacuil, nochinancal.

67. la mar. 68. alborotar o remouer. p̃. onicolini.

69. hĩchar. p̃. onicteponaço. 70. hazer heruir el agua.

Variously they named the sheet lightning or thunder bolts. They attributed them to the Tlalocs or *tlamacazque*. They said that these made the thunderbolts and sheet lightning and peals of thunder, and [that] they smote with them whomsoever they would.

Por diuersos nombres nonbran al relampago o rayo atribuyãle a los tlaloques o tlamacaces. Dezian que ellos hazian los rayos y relampagos y truenos y ellos herian con ellos a quien querian.

Fifth Chapter

Clouds and rain these natives attributed to a god whom they called Tlalocan tecutli, who had many other [gods] under his command, who were named Tlalocs and *tlamacazque*. These [people] thought that they created all things needed for the body, such as maize and beans, etc.; and that they sent the rains so that all things growing in the earth would

Las nubes y las pluuias atribuianlas estos naturales a vn dios que llamauan tlaloca tecutli, el qual tenia muchos otros debaxo de su dominio a los quales llamauan tlaloque y tlamacazque. Estos pensauan que criauan todas las cosas necesarias pa el cuerpo como mayz y frisoles etc. Y que ellos embiauan las pluuias para que naciesen todas las cosas que se crian

p̃. onicpoçonalti. onicpoçoni. 71. Causar olas en el agua o leuantarlas. p̃. onicacuecuenyoti. 72. hazer estruendo las olas que quiebran. p̃. otetecuicatimãca. ococomocatimanca. 73. arrojar en alto. p̃. onicacomayauh. onicacotlaz.

1. tlapetlanillotl. tlapetlaniliztli. much ic quino-
2.   3.
tzaya. quitocayotiaya ayauhcocolli. tlapetlanilquauitl
[4.]   5.
oztopilquauitl. Yn iquac tlapetlani, tlatlapetlani, tix-
6.   7.
poyaua, tixmimiqui. titixmauhtia, titocuitiuetzi.
8.   9.
Ayxnamiquiliztli, aixnamiquiztli, noviyã tlatlaneztimoquetza, yuhquin tlauizcalli moquequetza. Ynic
10.   10.
vallauh valcocoliuhtiuh. cuecueliuhtiuitz.

1. Relampago. 2. niebla o esalacion que va culebreando. 3. rayo. 4. relampaguear. p̃. otlapetlan. otlatlapetlan. 5. perder la vista. p̃. onixpoyaua. onixmimic. 6. obfuscarse la uista. p̃. oninixmauhti. 7. estremecerse. p̃. oninocuitiuetz. 8. Cosa en que se puede poner la vista. 9. aparecer gran claridad. p̃. otlatlaneztimoq̃tz. otlauizcalli moquequetz. 10. venir culebreando. p̃. oualcocoliuhtia. oualcueliuhtia.

1. Tlaloca tecutli.
2.   3.
Teutl ypan machoya, ytech tlamiloya yn quiauitl yn
4.   5.
atl, yuh quitouaya yeh quichiua yn ticqua, ỹ tiqui,
6.   7.   8.   8.   8.
yn qualoni, yn iuani, yn tonẽca, yn toyolca, yn to-
8.   8.   9.
cochca, yn toneuhca, yn tocemilhuitiaya yn tonaca-
10.   11.
yotl, in ye ixquich xopanyotl yn itzmolintoc ỹ
11.   12.   13.   14.   15.
celiztoc, yn quilitl, ỹ vauhtli, yn chian, yn ayotetl,

1. El dios de su payso terrenal. el dios de las nubes. o el dios se las lluuias. truenos nublados. 2. atribuir. pres. tetech nictlamia. p̃. tetech onictlami. 3. lluuia. 4. comer. p̃. onitlacua. 5. beuer. p̃. oniquic. onitlai. 6. Cosa comestible. 7. cosa buena pa beuer. 8. Cosa para sustentar la vida. 9. mantenimiento. o bastimento. ca. notonacayouh. 10. las cosas que se hazen

73

burst forth. And when they observed the feast of this god and his subjects, before the celebration, those whom they called *tlamacazque* (who lived in the temple house named *calmecac*) fasted four days. And, the fast concluded, if there were a malefactor among them, in honor of those gods they mishandled him in the lake, dragging and kicking him through the mire and through the water.

en la tierra. Y quando hazian fiesta a este dios y a sus subiectos antes de la fiesta ayunauã quatro dias aquellos que llamauan tlamacazque los quales morauan en la casa del templo llamada calmecac. Y acabado el ayuno si algun malhechor entre ellos avia por honrra de aquellos dioses le maltratauan en la laguna arrestrandole y acozeandole por el cieno y por el agua.

yn etl, ỹ metl, yn nopalli, yoan yn oc cequi yn amo

21.   22.   23.   24.

qualoni, ỹ xochitl, ỹ xiuitl. Auh yn iꝗc ylhuiquixti-

liloya, achtopa navilhuitl moçavaya, motlalocaçauaya

25.   26.   27.

yn tlamacazque, ỹ moteneua calmecac movapaua,

27.   28.

mozcaltia. Yn iquac oacic navilhuitl, in ye neualco,

29.   29.

in yeilhuitl muchiua, matlãpapachoaya mopopolac-

30.   31.

tiaya in vey apan, amo yviyan, amo motlamachuia ỹ

32.   33.

atlan õmotzotzopontitlaça, õmotzotzopontimayaui,

34.   35.   36.   37.

çã monetechuia vncan çoquitlan quinemitia, quipopo-

38.   39.   40.

lactia, quiuilana, ycpac cantinemi. quititilicça. atlan

41.   41.   42.

tlatzotzopotztinemi. aycoxochtinemi. tlamoMolotzti-

43.

nemi ỹmac mouiuitlatinemi ỹ tlamacazque yn otla-

44.   45.

tlaco. yn calmecac ytlã oncholo. Yntlanel çan aca

46.   47.   48. 49. 50.

õmotepotlami, ytla oconicxixopeuh. ocuel yc onaci-

51. 52.   53.

que. ye ic ỹmal ça quipipie, aocmo conixcaua ynic

54.   55.   56.

catlampapachozque. Auh amo çã quenin quipoloa,

57.   57.   58.

vel quicocoltia, quellelaxitia, çã quẽ quimattoc, ça

59.   60.   61.   62.

mopopoçauhtoc, ça yçomocatoc, ça micqui yn quiual-

63.   64.   65.   66.

mayaui atenco: ayac vel ypan tlatoa, vncan quimon-

67.   68.

ana yn intahuã yn ĩnanvan. Auh yn aquin quitla-

mauhcayttilia yn quitlatẽmachilia ypiltzin, ynic amo

69.   70.

catlampapachozque conquixtiaya, ytlatzin quĩma-

71.   72.   73.

caya yn tlamacazque, aço totolin, aço tlaqualli: yc

74.   75.

quicavaya. Auh yn iquac hin, ỹ noviyan techachan ỹ

el tp̃o de las aguas. 11. estar nacido alguna cosa verde como flor o yerua. o oja de arbol. p̃. oytzmolintoca. oceliztoca. 12. verdura pa comer. caso. noquil. 13. cenizos. ca. nouauh. 14. vna yerua en que se haze vna semilla como linaça. ca. nochie. nochiã. 15. calabança. ca. nayoteuh. nayo. 16. frisoles. ca. neuh. 17. magueyes. ca. nomeuh. 18. ojas de tonales. ca. nonopal. 19. otras cosas. 20. no comestible. 21. flores. ca. noxochiuh. 22. yerua. ca. noxiuh. 23. y quando. 24. hazer fiesta. p̃. onilhuiquixti. hazer fiesta a alguno. p̃. oniteilhuiquixtili. 25. ministros del templo. rec. tlamacazqui. 26. la casa del templo donde morauan los que seruian al templo. 27. criarse. p̃. oninovapauh. oninozcalti. 28. en el fin del ayuno. 29. meter debaxo del agua al que quiere salir del agua. p̃. oniteatlampapacho. onitepopolac. 30. en la mar. rec. Vey atl. 31. hazer algo con templança o con asosiego. p̃. onitetlamachui. 32. en el agua. 33. çabulir. o çapuçar en el agua. p̃. onitetzopontitlaz. onitetzopontimayauh. 34. hazer algo vnos a otros los que son de vn mismo linaje. o de vn mismo vando. o de vna misma religion maltratandose o des. . . . . . dose los vnos a los otros. p̃. otitotechuique. careçe de singular. 35. en el lodo. recto. çoquitl. 36. traer algo

And if he tried to rise, by force they again pushed him under the water, until they almost drowned him. They who, in the house called *calmecac,* committed some fault—like breaking some vessel, or some such thing—these they seized and kept under guard in order to punish them on that day. And sometimes the parents of him who was thus detained gave chickens or capes or other things to the priests so that they would let [him] go and not drown [him]. To those whom they thus illtreated, neither their parents nor their kin dared show favor nor speak for them, if previously they had not freed them while they were imprisoned; and so badly did they treat [the victims] that they even left them almost for dead cast on the brink of the water. Then their parents took them up and carried them to their houses. In this feast of these gods, all the common folk ate maize boiled like rice. And the priests went dancing and singing through the streets. In one hand they carried a stalk of green maize, and in the other a pot with a handle. In this way they went asking that [the householders] give them boiled maize. And all the common folk cast that boiled maize into the pots which they carried.

y si se queria leuantar tornauãle por fuerça, a meter debaxo del agua hasta que casi le ahogauã. Los que en la casa llamada calmecac hazian algun defecto como es quebrar alguna basija o cosa semejante los prendian y tenian guardados para castigallos aquel dia. Y algunas vezes los padres del que asi estaua preso daban galinas, o mantas o otras cosas a los tlamacaces porque lo soltasen y no le ahogasen. A los que maltratauã desta manera ni sus padres ni sus parientes osauan favorecellos ni hablar por ellos si antes no los avian librado estãdo presos y tanto los maltratauã hasta que los dexauã casi por muertos arrojados a la orilla del agua. Entonces los tomauan sus padres y los lleuauan a sus casas. En esta fiesta destos dioses todos los maceuales comian mayz cozido hecho como arroz. Y los tlamacaces andauan baylando y cantando por las calles en vna mano trayan vña caña de mayz verde y en otra vna olla con asa por este modo andauã demandando que les diesen mayz cozido y todos los maceuales les echauan en las ollas que trayan de aquel mayz cozido.

75. 76. 77. 78.
cecencalpan etzalqualoya, cecēyaca metzalhuiaya.
79. 80. 81. 82.
yoan etzalmacevaloya, cintopiltica mitotia, tepan ca-
83. 83. 84.
calaqui, motlatlaeuia, motlatlaytlania yn etzalma-
85. 86. 87. 88.
ceuhque, çã mucheh yn etzalli quīmaca ȳ xoxocvicol,
89. 90.
ymeetzalcon yntlan caana./

de aca paralla. p̃. onitenen. 37. çabulir algo debaxo
del agua. p̃. onitepolacti. 38. arrastrar persona.
pre. oniteuilã. 39. traer alguno de los cabellos por
fuerça. p̃. teicpac onitean. 40. dar de cozes a alguno.
p̃. onitetitilicçac. 41. andar reboluiendo el agua andando debaxo della. p̃. onitlatzotzopotztine. onaico-
xotztine. 42. hazer heruir el agua cõ el mouimiento
que haze el que anda debaxo della. p̃. onitlamomo-
lotztine. 43. escabullirse de las manos de los que le
quieren tomar. p̃. temac oninouiuitlatinẽ. 44. hazer
algun defecto, como quebrar algo. o trastornar algo.
p̃. ytla ononcholo. pro ytla onoconitlaco. 45. avnque
algun. 46. tropeçar. pres. ninotepotlamia. 47. dar
punta de pie a alguna cosa. pres. nitlacxixopeua.
48. luego. 49. por esta causa. 50. prender. p̃s. nicaci.
p̃. onicacic. 51. presionero. rec. malli. 52. poner cerco
para guardar a algun que no se pueda huyr. pre.
onitepipix. 53. tener los ojos puestos en algũa psona
para que no se escapulla. p̃. amo oniq'xcauh. 54.
hazer aquel maltratamj.° en el agua a aquellos que
ansi castigauan. p̃. oniteatlampapacho. 55. demasi-
adamente. 56. dar tarea de cozes o mesones. p̃.
onitepolo. 57. fatigar. o afligir. p̃. onitecocolti. oniteel-
lelaxiti. 58. estar a punto de muerte. p̃. ça quẽ

They said that these gods made the clouds, the rains, and hail, snow, peals of thunder, sheet lightning, and thunderbolts.

Estos dioses dezian que hazian las nubes y las lluuias, y el granizo, y la nieue, y los truenos y los relampagos y los rayos.

The rainbow is something like an arch of hewn stone. It showeth divers colors. When it appeareth, it is a sign of clear weather.

El arco del cielo es a manera de arco de canteria tiene aparencia de diuersos colores. quando aparece es señal de serenidad.

Jn yehoantin hī moteneua tlaloque yntech tlamiloya ȳ mixtli, yn quiauitl, yn teciuitl, ȳ cepayauitl, yn ayauitl yn tlapetlaniliztli, yn tlatlatziniliztli, yn teuitequiliztli.

onicmattoca. 59. anelar con gran angustia. p̄. oninopopoçauhtoca. 60. estar azezando como de muerte. p̄. oniçomocatoca. 61. el que esta a punto de morir. 62. arrojar algo. p̄. onicmayauh. 63. ninguno. 64. fauorecer. p̄. tepan onitlato. 65. de alli. 66. tomar algo. p̄. onicā. 67. Y si alguno. 68. temer el mal q̃ a de venir a otro. p̄. onitetlamauhcaittili. onitetlatenmachili. 69. sacar. o librar. p̄. onitequixti. 70. alguna cosa. 71. gallina. ca. nototol. 72. comida. ca. notlaqual. 73. por esta causa. 74. dexar. p̄. oniccauh. 75. en todas las casas. 76. comer mayz cozido. 77. cada psona. 78. hazer pa si mayz cozido. p̄. oninetzalhui. 79. baylar demandando el mayz cozido por calles. 80. con cañas de mayz verde. rec. cintopilli. ca. nocītopil. 81. bailar. p̄. oninitoti. 82. entrar de casas en casa. p̄. tepan onicacalac. 83. demãdar limosna. p̄. oninotlatlaeui. oninotlatlaitlani. 84. los bayladores q̃ demandã mayz cozido. 85. todos lo mismo. 86. el mayz cozido como arroz. ca. netzal. 87. dar. p̄. onictemacac. 88. olla con asa. rec. xocvicolli. 89. olla de mayz cozido. rec. etzalcomitl. 90. lleuar algo colgado de la mano. p̄. notlan onican.

1. Ayauhcoçamalotl.
<pre>   2.   3.   3.</pre>
Yuhquin vitoliuhqui tlauitoltic. coltic ynic valmo-
<pre>   4.   4.</pre>
quetza. tlatlatlapalpoalli, motlatlapalpouh yn itla-

2. cosa arcuada, o hecha a manera de arco. 3. cosa corua. 4. cosa pintada de diuersos colores. 5. cosa verde. 6. verdescuro. 7. cosa amarilla. 8. cosa de color

And when the rainbow fixeth itself over a maguey, they said it would cause [the plant] to dry or wither. And they also said that when the rainbow appeareth often, it is a sign that the season of rain is about to cease.

y quando de arco del cielo se pone sobre algun maguey dezian que le haria secar o marchitar. Y tanbiẽ dezian que quando espesas vezes aparece el arco del cielo, es señal que ya quieren cesar las aguas.

chieliz ỹ centlamantli tlapalli ytech neci xoxoctic,
6.   6.   6.   6.   6.
quiltic, quilpaltic, iyappaltic, quilpalli, iyappalli:
7.   8.   8.   9.
yoan coztic, xopaltic, xochipalli, niman ye chichiltic
9.   10.   10.   11.
tlapaltic, yoan tlaztaleualtic, tlazteleualli, yoan texo-
11.   12.   12.
tic, texotli, matlaltic, matlalli. Auh quitoa yn iq̄c
13.   14.   15.
valmoquetza, quinextia, quiteittitia, quinezcayotia,
16.   16.   17.   18.
yc macho, yc machizti yc itto yn amo quiauiz, amo
19.   19.   20.
tlaelquiauiz, amo tilauaz, ça quimomoyava ỹ mixtli,
21.   22.   23.
quipopoloa, quelleltia, quiyacatzacuilia yn quiauitl,
24.   25.   25.
yn tlaelquiauitl yn tepaltilli, yn techaquani, ỹ te-
26.   27.
çoq'tili. Yntla cenca omotlatlali mixtli, yn ovel cui-
27.
cuicheuac, ynonoviyan tlâtlayouac, çan quipopoloa.
28.
Yntlanel quiaui, aocmo cenca tilaua, aocmo molhuia,
29.   30.   31.
ça auachquiaui, auachtli yn onveuetzi, yn onchichi-
32.   32.   32.
pini, auachpitzactli, avachpicilli, auachauachpicilto-
34.   35.   36.
ton yn ontzitzicuini, yn onveuetzi: anoceh çan avach-
37.   37.
tilaua, avachtilauatimani, auachtzetzeliuhtimani.

Auh quitoa quilmach yntla metl ypan moquetza, yc
38.   39.   40.
macueçaliciui, macoçauia, mauaqui, machichiliui,
41.
matlatlauia, macuetlauia. No yoan quitoa yn iquac
42.
miecpa valmoquetza yc neci çã cuel quiçaz yn quia-
43.
vitl, quitoaya çan cuel yazque yn avaque, ye quiçazque yn tlaloque.

naranjada o leonada. 9. cosa colorada. 10. cosa mo-
rada o encarnada. 11. cosa azul. 12. cosa de color de
cardenil o cosa azul. 13. demostrarse. o leuantarse.
p̄. ovalmoquetz. oualnez. 14. demostrar. p̄. onicnexti.
onicteittiti. 15. significar o p̄nosticar. p̄. onicnezca-
yoti. 16. saber p̄. omachoc. omachiztic. 17. ser visto.
p̄. oyttoc. 18. llouer. p̄s. quiaui. p̄. oquiauh. 19. llouer
mucho. p̄s. tlaelquiaui. p̄. otlaelquiauh. otilauh. 20.
derramar. p̄. onicmomoyauh. 21. desbaratar. p̄. onic-
popolo. 22. impedir o estoruar. p̄. oniquellelti. 23.
atajar. p̄. onicyacatzacuili. 24. aguazero. 25. cosa que
moja. 26. ponerse nublados. 27. ponerse oscuridad
por razon de muchos nublados. pres. cuicuicheua,
tlatlayoua. 28. hazerse algo reziamēte. p̄. oninolhui
29. lluuiznar. p̄. oauachquiauh. 30. hazer molizna.
p̄. auachtli ōueuetz. 31. caer algunas gotas de agua.
p̄. onchichipin. 32. molizna. 34. ruziar con alguna
cosa. p̄. ontzitzicuī. 35. caer. p̄. onveuetz. 36. moliz-
near. pret.º oauachtilauac. 37. estar molizneando.
38. pararse lo uerde amarillo en disposiciō de secarse.
p̄. omacueçaliciuh. omacoçauix. 39. secarse las ramas.
p̄. omauac. 40. pararse las ramas coloradas. p̄. omachi-
chiliuh. omatlatlauix. 41. marchitarse las ramas. p̄.
omacuetlauix. 42. de presto. o prestamente. 43. los
señores de la pluuia.